I0467578

How To Make Money on eBay - Maximize Profits

Secrets, Stories, Tips and Hacks - Confessions of a 16-year eBay Veteran

Jill b.

ISBN: 1534745068
ISBN-13: 978-1534745063

CONTENTS

IMPORTANT :

When you are buying items from a retailer,

NEVER MENTION THIS BOOK, OR THAT YOU ARE RESELLING YOUR PURCHASE ON EBAY/AMAZON.

Doing so will likely ruin your source. Corporate/store policy may change. Please do not ruin it for yourself and everyone else.

Do not brag, be polite, and keep a low profile. If you need to, say you stock up on Christmas presents when you see a deal.

1 WHAT THIS BOOK IS AND IS NOT ABOUT

This book is not an "eBay for Dummies" book. It is not a book for beginners. I will not show you how to set up your eBay and paypal account, nor how to take good photos nor how you should title your auctions. There are many other books out there that cover that. You can probably look up such information for free on Google, eBay, and/or Paypal.

Some sections of the book may not apply to you, depending on your individual risk tolerance or where you live. Some ideas can be applied to selling on Amazon too. I have sold many items on Amazon as well, but Amazon is a different beast. My focus will be selling on eBay. Some ideas are universal, regardless of where you are in the world, but the details in most of this book will apply only to US-based sellers.

I will not promise that you will get rich on eBay, nor will I promise that you will be able to quit your job. I will not tell you I only work 2 hours a day and make $5000 per month selling on eBay. While you can work only 2 hours a day on eBay as a sideline, chances are you will not be making $5000 per month through eBay sales. You can make eBay a hobby, but if you want it to be a business, you will have to run it like a business.

I am not a fan of purchasing at wholesale level to resell and I will not give you vague recommendations to buy "stuff" from unspecified wholesale suppliers to resell on eBay. I will not try to sell you anything (other than this book). Any suggestions and recommendations are based on my personal experiences. I am not affiliated in any way with the companies I discuss in the book, nor do I receive any compensation for any of my suggestions. My recommendations are based solely on my personal experiences. Information provided is accurate to the best of my knowledge at the time of writing.

As a 16-year professional eBay seller, I will not give you a list of items that I think currently sells and tell you to go on Craigslist to look for said items. I will not claim to be an "expert". If there is one thing I have learned on eBay it is that nothing is constant or certain. What sells one day may not sell the next. Instead, I will provide you with the *tools* to source for items to sell, as well as tips on how to maximize your profits.

These are tools that I have acquired in the course of my making a full-time living on eBay, since 1998. Like any other tool, how useful it is will depend on whose hands the tool ends up in. As with everything else, things change. You will need to update the tools I provide you over time by keeping yourself up-to-date with relevant developments.

Again, this book is not a get-rich quick scheme. Can you get rich on eBay? Maybe. Can you quit your job and sell full-time? Possibly. Can you make a side-income from selling online? Most probably. Everyone's path is different.

Economies and currencies rise and fall. Technologies change. Trends and customers come and go. If there's one thing I learned in my years of selling on eBay is that nothing is a sure thing. Something that sold for $600 one day might only sell for $100 the next, the demand dies out and you are stuck with your stock. The beauty of being an eBay seller is that you are small and nimble enough to be able to change your business to suit the current eBay environment.

Why am I revealing my secrets now? What's in it for me? My life has changed a lot since my college days in 1998, when I first started selling on eBay. I now have a family and my priorities have shifted. With an impending move further into the countryside, I am looking into more passive income sources like selling books I have written. Please feel free to visit me at http://byjillb.com for a full list of homesteading and natural living books.

In this book, I will reveal my closely guarded secrets. Looking back, I really did not need to guard my "secrets" that closely. The world is an abundant selling opportunity. No one can be everywhere at every time to sell everything on eBay. Selling on eBay is a fun ride. I hope you'll find this book very helpful in your eBay endeavors!

2 WHO I AM - A LITTLE HISTORY

What makes me different from other authors of How-To eBay books? Most notably, I have made a full time living on eBay since 1998. I was one of the pioneering Powersellers and Top Rated Sellers. With the help of my mother in Singapore, who helped to pack and ship orders (while she held a full-time job).

By the time I graduated in 2001, I was able to sell enough merchandise on eBay to pay for the final two years of my college education. I did all this while attending college full-time *and* having a part-time job at school. In case you're wondering, I did still get 6-8 hours of sleep a day! Of course, I could never have done anything without my mother's help from halfway around the world. I have never had a "real" full-time job since graduating with an Engineering degree from Cornell University.

Here is a sampling of my eBay experience:

I have sold just about anything: anime, all kinds of memorabilia (from video games to movies), postcards, toys (new and vintage), vintage items, cosmetics, food, jewelry, books, magazines, electronics in every shape and form, TVs, DVDs, video games, gemstones, Louis Vuitton bags, stickers, computer parts, software, household and kitchen appliances, clothing and even a car!

Countries where I have traveled to and found items to sell: Singapore (my home country), US (my adopted country),

Canada, Hungary, Japan, China, Thailand, The Netherlands, Germany, Hong Kong and the UK.

Places I have shipped eBay orders *from*: Singapore, Calgary (Canada), Bangkok (Thailand), New York, New Mexico, Colorado and California.

Additionally, I have shipped countless items *to* all 50 states, as well as to many countries in six continents including the main English *and* French-speaking countries, Italy, Germany, Brazil, Peru, Ecuador, Saudi Arabia, the UAE, Israel, South Africa, Malaysia, China, Thailand, Taiwan, Hungary, Austria, all the Scandinavian countries, Russia and Turkey to name a few off the top of my head.

Selling on eBay today is quite different from when I first started selling on the site in 1998. I was a sophomore at Cornell, looking for ways to make extra money from my dorm room. Then, I found this site called eBay - it was then an online auction-only site that became popular with Pez dispensers collectors.

I wanted to try my hand at selling on eBay but I did not know what to sell. While on vacation back home in Singapore, I did quite a bit of research (by checking completed listings) and found that there was a small niche market within eBay for magazines featuring Asian actresses like Gong Li.

I took advantage of my being able to have a foot in both the US market and having access to Singapore magazines. I started risk-free, by scouring each floor of my whole apartment block, collecting TV Guides that people had put out for recycling.With no overheads other than the eBay listing fees, I made decent profits and was itching to expand my product line.

As money rolled in, my mum invested in a photo scanner for me. Back then, digital cameras were very expensive. We would take photos of products with our film camera, get them developed, then scan and upload the scanned photos onto eBay. Paypal or its predecessor, x.com had not been launched yet. Buyers would have to send payment via check, money order or in many cases, cash in the mail.

The feedback system was extremely important because buyers had to trust you to ship to them. I remember payments often arriving in my mailbox in the form of wads of cash. Times have certainly changed!

I then invested in Pez dispensers which was a miserable failure - I think the bag of Pez's are still sitting somewhere in my parents' apartment. Then I found a new market - Anime. Anime was starting to get very popular in the US at a time that stores in Singapore were clearing out their stocks of old anime items including Dragonball Z toys. Toys I had purchased for as little as S$1 (~US$0.70) would sell on eBay for US$30-US$50. *CA-CHING!*

I was lucky to be at the crossroads of two economies. In 1998, East Asian countries, including Singapore were still licking their wounds from the 1997 Asian financial crisis. The economy was depressed. In the US however, the economy was booming. I was at the forefront of a (growing anime) trend at a time when people were flush with cash and willing to spend gobs of it on anything novel on eBay.

I also had the upper hand against other Singaporean sellers since I had an address and a bank account in New York where I could receive and deposit all those checks and wads of cash.

People felt safer sending payments to someone in the States versus sending cash to someone halfway across the world. Then, Paypal came along and eventually, more sellers started flooding the market. Over time, this niche market eventually dried up.

Since then, I've been through the Dot-Com Crash and the Great Recession. At the time of writing this book, the economy still hasn't quite recovered yet. I have been through many eBay fee hikes, postal shipping hikes and tightened eBay rules.

But, you can still make money on eBay. How? You may be asking. You can simply harness eBay and the internet to take advantage of arbitrage. I will talk more about arbitrage in a later chapter.

3 STARTING YOUR EBAY/ONLINE BUSINESS

You can simply start your eBay business with your personal information and social security number (for paypal). It is OK to run your business as a sole proprietor if you are just planning on selling one or two items on eBay occasionally.

The following suggestions are for informational purposes only. These are the steps that I have taken with my business. I am not a lawyer or tax professional. You should consult your local legal and tax professional if you need specific advice about setting up your business.

If you're planning on selling on eBay with any kind of seriousness, you might want to consider setting up a separate company entity, preferably a limited liability corporation (LLC). You can register your corporate entity status through your Secretary of State's website.

Once you have a business established through your state, you can apply for an Employer Identification Number (EIN) though the IRS (http://1.usa.gov/1hBUiLt). An EIN is a tax identification number which is separate from your personal social security number.

The process can be done for free online and the process is quick and easy. The IRS will issue you an EIN almost immediately. I suggest using your EIN for all your business transactions including your paypal and business bank account information. You will also use your EIN when you file tax returns for the business.

Finally, if your state charges sales tax, register for a resale license or certification. You should be able to find the information on your Secretary of State's website as well. Each state has its own process for issuing resale licenses. Sales tax rates can run to over 9% in some states. Basically, the state will issue documentation which you provide to your supplier. With that, your supplier will waive the sales tax on the item(s) you purchase from them. In turn, you will have to collect sales tax from your buyer when they purchase the item from you.

You only collect sales tax from buyers within the state you are located in. By purchasing inventory or supplies in this manner, you will save yourself the sales tax you would otherwise have incurred. Again, my suggestions are based on my experiences reselling from Colorado and New Mexico. You should contact your local tax and/or business professional if you need current or specific help or advice.

Now that you have set everything up, you can proceed to set up your accounts on eBay and paypal. You can follow the instructions on each site to set up your accounts. I will not go into the details as the process is straightforward and may change over time.

To sell on eBay you will need to have a computer with internet access. I also suggest investing in a digital shipping scale, and a digital camera (if you already have a digital camera in a phone or other device that works as well). A smartphone will make your life easier but it is not necessary unless you're starting to make a decent profit. If you do have a smartphone, be sure to download the eBay app (http://mobile.ebay.com/) - it will make listing auctions and looking up product trends easier while you are out and about.

4 SHIPPING

I will discuss shipping first because it is a crucial component of selling on eBay. Knowing the logistics of shipping any product you find to sell on eBay will be important in deciding whether or not the item you have found will be suitable for sale online.

I personally avoid dealing with bulky and/or very heavy items. Shipping and packing such items pose too many problems for me. Unless you live in a major metropolitan area, your orders from eBay will very rarely be a local pickup. Such items are better listed for sale on sites such as Craiglist.org (the response from Craigslist will depend on your location, especially to your proximity to a metropoliation area).

One thing I suggest you invest in, even if you're just starting out, is a digital shipping scale. You can purchase one from Staples at a lower cost using my Staples buying tricks. Refer to the Staples Chapter for more information.

In order to list items for sale without ending up on the losing end of the bargain because you mis-estimated shipping charges, you must know beforehand how much your shipping cost for that item is going to be. Knowing how much your shipping cost is going to be will help you decide if you can afford to offer free shipping, if you can offer flat rate shipping, or if you will use calculated shipping charges.

Free Shipping, Calculated Shipping or Flat-Rate Shipping?

If your item is small and light (13 oz or under), and you have a healthy profit margin, you can opt to offer free domestic shipping. For the last few years, eBay has been pressuring sellers to offer free shipping. Do not feel forced into something you are not comfortable with. If you offer free shipping, you will actually have to roll your shipping costs into your item price to avoid losing money.

As of 2014, the USPS charges under $4.50 to ship a 13 oz package across the US via first class mail. Therefore, you can easily lose money by selling a 13 oz item you purchased for $5 and sold for $10 with free shipping.

Here is how you lost money:

Sale price with free shipping: $10
Item cost: $5
Shipping cost to ship a 13 oz package across the country: $4.12
eBay fee: $1 (10% commision)
Paypal fee: $0.30 + 2.9% = $0.59
Total cost: $10.71
Total **loss** = $0.71 + anything else you spent on packing materials

Rates change and usually increase every year so check USPS.com for current rates.

If you are starting out, I suggest you charge shipping rates based on calculated shipping charges. That way, you can just focus on your item's profit margin when you're determining your price without getting confused with the shipping costs that you will need to factor into your price if you offered free shipping.

eBay charges fees (currently a 10% commission) on any shipping charges that you include. Under "shipping charges", eBay will allow you to charge postage based on the calculated rate. All you need to do is to input the weight of your package (remember to include the weight of your packaging: box, packing material etc, as well as all shipping services will charge you a price based on the final total weight of your package).

Weigh your packaged items then enter the weight into eBay's system. eBay will then charge your buyer the appropriate postage charges based on weight, package size and destination, less any bonus shipping discounts they may have at that time. This is a good way to figure out shipping charges especially if you're starting out on eBay. Additionally, eBay will automatically update shipping charges if and when the USPS increases their rates annually.

If you use eBay's "calculated shipping charge" option, eBay will also allow you to add a handling charge. You can set your handling charge to $0. Or, you may wish to add an additional small fee to cover costs like packing materials, labor to ship and pack, and mileage to drop off your packages at your shipping location.

Be reasonable with your handling charges because charging too much will turn buyers away from your listings. Personally, I prefer to pad the item's shipping weight by a few ounces to help defray the handling costs and eBay fees. I also normally add a handling fee of $1-$2 for international shipments because of the added costs/hassles (paypal for example, will add an additional cross-border fee transaction).

Finally, eBay gives you the option of charging buyers a "flat-rate" shipping charge. Again, they will charge you their commission on your shipping charge. Basically, you charge all buyers within a certain country a flat-rate. You can also charge different flat-rate fees to buyers in Canada and to other countries outside North America. You can refer to http://postcalc.usps.com/ for current USPS rates.

If you are listing products in certain categories, such as movies, video games and books (items that can be shipped at a much lower cost under USPS media rates), eBay limits the shipping charge amount that you are allowed to charge buyers.

I do not recommend flat-rate calculations if you are not familiar with shipping processes and costs. Even I, with all my years of selling experience, have been hit with unexpected shipping costs when I miscalculated shipping prices. It happens mostly during the time when the USPS makes their annual rate change (usually in January of the new year).

After your buyer has paid for your sale, eBay makes things easy for you. You can print USPS or Fedex labels directly from your eBay account. Under "my eBay" and "sold items", you can see what you have sold and print shipping labels for them. If you used "calculated shipping" in your listing, eBay will automatically calculate your postage fees based on the shipping weight which you originally entered in your listing.

If you padded the weight of your package, remember to correct the weight of the item before purchasing your shipping label.

You can pay for the shipping charges directly through paypal. eBay streamlines the process for you. There are no additional fees for this service. In fact, at the time of writing, eBay offers two nice extras: the actual postage amount paid is hidden, and they offer shipping discounts for printing labels though the site.

Considering Other Shipping Options Can Save You Postage Costs

USPS Priority Mail vs Parcel Post

If your package is 13 oz or under, I've found that USPS first class mail is the cheapest shipping option. Any shipment that is over 13 oz has to be shipped via Parcel Post, or via Priority or Express Mail. Parcel Post is supposed to be the more economical option.

However, you should be careful. If your package is between 14 oz - 3 lbs and/or you are shipping to an address that is within your state or within the neighboring states two states,

Priority Mail is often cheaper or similar in price to Parcel Post rates.

It is usually worth double checking Priority Mail rates before assuming it costs more than Parcel Post. Sometimes Priority Mail is cheaper, sometimes it costs only a few cents more than Parcel Post. If any of these two cases apply, use Priority Mail because the USPS will provide you with free boxes, packing tape and (domestic) insurance with the Priority Mail rate.

I think the extra few cents in cost is worth all the extras that Priority Mail provides. You can order free supplies at http://1.usa.gov/1DtFj27. You can also get these free supplies from your local post office.

When you are researching Priority Mail options, do not forget to see if you can save money using the USPS's flat rate services. Flat-rate Priority Mail services are available if you have shipments that can fit into their flat-rate envelopes or boxes.

The USPS will let you ship domestic packages up to 70 lbs (up to 4 lbs for international shipments) for one flat rate as long as it fits into their flat-rate packages. The package cannot be altered. You can potentially save a lot of money on shipping using this service.

I have squeezed amazing volumes of items into flat-rate envelopes. Sometimes it takes a little bit of finessing. If the envelope flap does not quite make it to the other side of the seal edge, place a piece of clean white paper over the "opening", then tape the seal and paper down using the

Priority Mail tape. The paper overlay both helps to keep the tape from sticking onto the item itself, and it helps make it less obvious that the package does not quite fit into the flat-rate envelope.

I admit that I have gotten evil looks at the post office when I present my super-stuffed envelopes, but they have always accepted them. Being nice and polite to your local post office clerk goes a long way!

Additionally, if you ship a Priority Mail package, you can have your mailman pick your package up from your doorstep (or another location of your choice at your address) for free, when he does his rounds.

You can schedule pick-ups online at http://1.usa.gov/1kNi08k as long as it is at least one day prior to the pick-up date. Click on "schedule a pickup" at (http://1.usa.gov/1kNi08k) to create your pickup day. If you are printing labels from eBay, you can also link to the pickup scheduling after you print a label. You can take advantage of this service as long as you have at least one Priority or Global Priority mail shipment to make.

Your mailman will pick up all your other ground shipments together with the Priority shipment. This is a nice service to have if you have a lot of large packages to ship that will not simply fit in your outgoing mailbox.

If you live in a rural or safe neighborhood, you should be able to just leave all your packages at the front door for pickup. I live in a safe rural Colorado mountain town so other than making sure my packages are safe from the weather, leaving packages unattended has not posed any problems for me. You can put your packages in free plastic buckets from the Post Office.

When I lived in New Mexico, I did not feel comfortable leaving my packages outside so I erred on the side of caution and had the mailman ring the doorbell for pickup. Do what you feel is comfortable to you.

Coming to your door to pick up (possibly) multitudes of heavy packages is extra work for your mail carrier, especially during the festive season. It might be nice to thanks them over the holidays with a nice card and perhaps a $10 gift card.

If you are shipping media items like printed materials, books, videos or CDs, you can ship your items via USPS media mail. As far as I know, this is the cheapest shipping option available to the small-time seller. Bear in mind that media mail shipping can be much slower than other postage services.

Video games do not qualify under the USPS's "media mail" criteria. You might be able to sneak some non-media mail items in media mail shipping past the USPS. However, every now and then, shipments may also come back to you for insufficient postage (delaying the arrival of the order), or worse, it may reach the addressee with postage due (customers have gotten mad and left negative feedback for this without prior notice to me). Ship non-media mail via media mail at your own risk!

Saving on Mailing Labels

eBay's free shipping label-printing service lets you print shipping labels right from their site. Under your sold listings, there will be a button next to each successful sale where you can "Print Shipping Label".

There are many advantages to using this service: you can hide the actual shipping charge, eBay often gives discounts over USPS rates, online tracking code is printed on the address label itself, and the buyer is automatically emailed the tracking number and is informed via email that the label for the order has been printed. I highly recommend that you use this service.

Remember: If you padded your shipping weight in your auction listing, as I suggested before, be sure to change it to the correct shipping weight before printing your label.

A point to note though, is that you can only print labels via eBay for packages. Packages are technically shipments that are over ¾" in height. For small, flat, cheap items like coupons or keychains or small figures that can fit in a regular envelope, it is cheaper to send it in a first-class envelope using postage stamps.

Here is an example: eBay charges $1.93 to ship a 1 oz package (with tracking) within the same zip code. At the time of writing, if you were to ship it using postage stamps, it would cost you $0.49 (if it is flat in a standard envelope) -$0.70 (if it is irregular). The only downside of using stamps is that you have no way of proving that you shipped the item. If the buyer complains to eBay that their order did not arrive, ebay will side with the customer and issue them a full refund at your expense. If the order is small enough, saving on the extra postage charges might be worth the risk.

I do not purchase special label printers or adhesive labels. Instead, I simply send the shipping labels to my regular printer. To save money (and to increase profits), I use the blank-side of used paper (make sure you do not have sensitive information on the other side), and I print using "grey-scale/draft/ink save mode".

You can find the ink save mode when your printer option pops out, go to "print or advanced properties" and choose "fast printing" or "draft printing" and print in black-and-white. The options will vary depending on your printer software.

To save on ink cost, I purchased a cheap Brother printer from Staples (I paid $0 out of pocket. The printer was priced at around $20 brand new - I will discuss how I get deals like this in my Staples section). In general, you can use generic inks for Brother printers.

You can purchase these generics for about $1 per ink cartridge from resellers on eBay or Amazon. Save your used cartridges (more on that later). I have used, and do not recommend HP printers. While you may be able to find deals on the printer itself, these printers use chipped HP ink cartridges which will add to your overhead costs.

Of course, if you are printing labels on plain paper, you will need to adhere it to your package using packing tape. You will need three strips of tape, stuck length-wise to stick the label on your package. Reduce your tape consumption by getting free plastic, customs envelopes (http://1.usa.gov/Z7pKO6) from USPS.

To reduce waste, I cut them in half and only use one-half per shipping label. The cut-side is then sealed to the package with a strip of packing tape. Using this method, you reduce your packing tape consumption by a third. Keep in mind that you can only use USPS supplies for USPS shipments. Do not use them for Fedex or UPS shipments. Both Fedex and UPS supply their own free shipping pouches.

You can use USPS plastic pouches to help to stick your paper-printed shipping labels to your package.
I have found that shipping flat items sandwiched this way is better than shipping it in a box.

Fedex and UPS

If the weight of your package is 4 lbs and above, and it does not fit into the USPS flat rate boxes, it is worth checking UPS and Fedex prices. One or both companies often offer more cost effective shipping options as compared to USPS if your packages are heavier.

You also get insurance up to $100 included in the cost. My recommendation is only valid for domestic shipments. International shipments via UPS or Fedex are expensive.

It is worth your while to sign up with both companies. Both often offer small business shipping discounts when you sign up for an account. Discount rates will vary depending on the promotion they have at that time.

Mailing Supplies

Mailing supplies which will include boxes, cushioning materials, packaging tape, mailing labels etc will all add to your final shipping costs. The only packing materials I purchase is bubble wrap and packing tape. All other supplies can normally be found for free.

Getting Free Boxes

A question that may crop up when you start out is, where do you get boxes? I do not buy shipping boxes nor do I recommend that you do so. I like to recycle boxes that arrive with my online orders. Save all those boxes that your orders come in! Do not keep any that are too crushed or damaged. If you have storage space to spare, leave the boxes as they are and store smaller boxes in bigger ones. Doing so not only helps you save on space and keep a little more organized, you can also see more quickly which box will work for your item. It is more time-consuming to figure out which box works best if your boxes are flattened down.

However, if you have limited storage space, break the usable boxes down and flatten them for easier storage. It is a good idea to organize them by size so that you can match your item to the appropriately sized box. An appropriately-sized box is one that your item fits in plus has enough space for a thin padding all around the item.

This box provides the adequate space for cushioning required for this shipment

If you do not make a lot of online purchases, good places to ask for free boxes of all shapes and sizes are big box craft stores like Hobby Lobby, or smaller grocery stores (I have never approached big box grocers like Walmart but I have not had problems approaching the staff at my local Safeway).

What kind of boxes do you look for? Always use boxes with firm, corrugated cardboard. Do not use flimsy one-layer cardboard. Also make sure that the cardboard used to make the boxes is not too thick.

While sturdy, thick cardboard boxes will add a lot of weight to your shipment and drive your shipping costs up. Big boxes constructed to hold heavy bulky items will be too thick for practical shipping use (unless of course, you are shipping heavy items).

If you are not sure what the difference is, just take heed from the shipping expert: Amazon. The thickness of the cardboard they use for their boxes will work for almost all your shipping needs. Do not use boxes that are unnecessarily big - it adds too much weight to your package and makes your item more susceptible to getting damaged because it will tend to roll around more in a large package.

If you are unable to find boxes of suitable sizes from these places, you can opt to make your own. Costco is a good place to get free large-sheets of corrugated cardboard. You do not need to be a member if you are not buying anything.

These cardboard sheets are used to separate their stacks of cereal boxes. Carefully remove the cardboard from between the cereal box stacks. Again, make sure you get the corrugated cardboard and not the one-layer cardboard. Both are used in their cereal aisle, depending on the brand. You should have no problems taking these out with you. I have never had anyone blink an eye when I take them. You can then fashion custom tubes and boxes out of these sheets.

Save Money - Make Your Own Poster Tubes

Poster tubes can be expensive to buy - at least $0.50 each for smaller ones IF you buy them in bulk. Save money by making your own tubes using free cardboard sheets from the Costco cereal isles.

Step 1: Cut your cardboard down to the appropriate length of your poster/shipment. Be sure to leave some space at the ends for cushioning.

Step 2: Give yourself enough cardboard widthwise to fashion a triangular tube PLUS an extra side for a more sturdy tube as so:

Step 3: Tape the edge of the cardboard down as so:

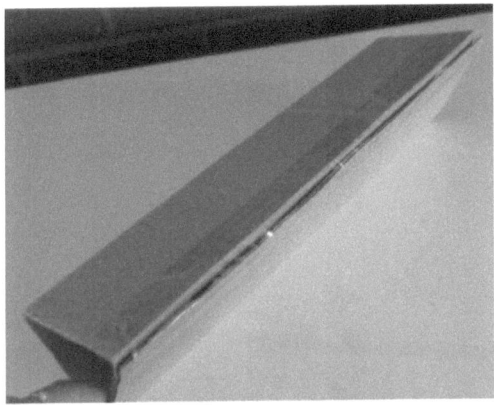

Step 4: Position your item in the tube, making sure there is some space leftover at each end for cushioning

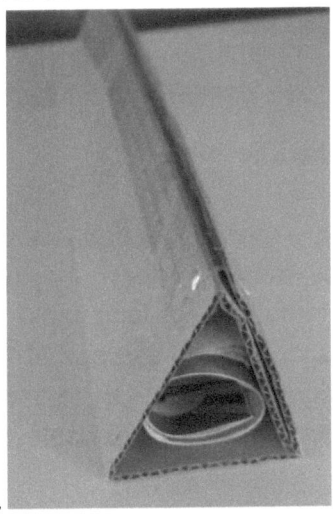

Step 5: Protect the ends with a small amount of balled up newspaper or clean plastic bags.

Step 6: Use packing tape to cover the entire end such that no part is exposed.

Step 7: Secure the tape edges by running a final strip of

packing tape around the edge of the tube.

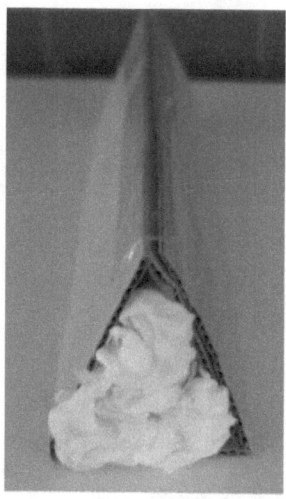

Trimming Off the Excess

Cardboard (and paper in general,) is unbelievably heavy. Save money by trimming down the inner box flaps (the shorter flaps - do not trim the long flaps). By trimming all four inner flaps you can save an average of 1 to 3 oz total - more if your box is bigger. Be sure not to trim it too close to the flap fold or you will render the box useless.

A rule of thumb will be to leave about 1" of inner flap for small boxes, leave about 3" for big boxes. That 1 oz may be the difference between being able to ship within the 13 oz first class category, or may mean that you do not get bumped up to the next pound weight category.

Cushioning Materials

Of course, you cannot ship your item in your box without cushioning - that is a sure way to have your item arrive damaged. For cushioning, you normally have the choice of peanuts, bubble wrap or air packs.

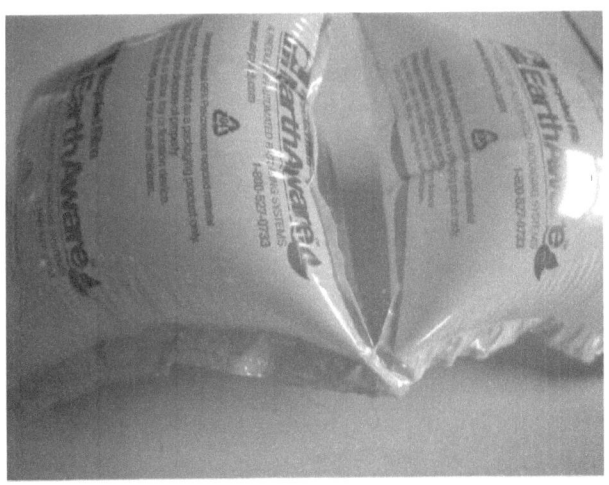

An example of air packs

Again, these normally come with any online orders. While I have used packing peanuts, I am not a fan of them. They are messy, hard to handle, and honestly, do not do a very good job of cushioning. Most shippers no longer use packing peanuts.

Instead, many have switched to air packs or bubble wrap. I like both, they are light and do a decent job of cushioning the product. Again, you can save these that may come in the mail but again, unlike boxes, they cannot be broken down for storage and can become bulky and unwieldy, especially if you have limited space.

If you do not have air bubble packs, an option will be to use loosely balled up newspaper as cushioning. Do not use magazine paper or worse, glossy magazine paper. Glossy paper is difficult to ball up and adds a *lot* more weight to the final shipment.

I credit my husband for this idea, and my personal recommendation is to use old plastic shopping bags - the kind of plastic bags you get from the grocery store. They are light and when balled up, they make good packing cushioning. Please be kind on the environment - use recycled bags. Also, please only use reasonably clean bags. Do not use bags that are wet, or funky in any way, or you might have problems with an angry buyer!

If you are concerned that your shipment will look unprofessional with your buyer, simply put this notice in all your auctions: "To help reduce environmental waste, and to help you save on shipping costs, please understand that I use recycled materials only. My recycling helps keep prices lower for my buyers." In all my years of selling online, I have never had complaints from buyers about my use of recycled packaging.

Bubble Mailers

I stopped using bubble mailers in my first year of selling on eBay. Instead of keeping a supply of bubble mailers of all sizes, I think it is better to invest in a large non-perforated roll of 3/16" bubble wrap. Wrap with 12" width works best for me and will adequately wrap most things like DVDs etc.

You can purchase 300' rolls from http://uline.com. Staples used to be the cheapest place to purchase large rolls but they seem to have discontinued it. Keep checking, who knows, it might come back in stock one day.

To package with a bubble roll, simply wrap the bubble wrap tightly around your item. One layer of wrap works fine for things like one to two disc DVDs and CDs. You might need two or three layers for larger box sets. Tape the bubble wrap down securely, making sure all sides are cushioned. If your wrap runs short, you can cut extra bubble strips to cover the exposed parts. Use the same number of layers as the rest of the package.

Finally, wrap kraft or butcher paper around the package. Taping all the sides together with packing tape is fine for smaller packages like DVDs. If you have bigger packages, you should also tape around the middle of the package both length and width-wise to prevent the wrapping paper from shredding too much during shipment.

If you are shipping something that is otherwise quite small like a keychain or gumball toy for example, you can tape a strip of bubble wrap around it and ship in a regular envelope.

This method of wrapping has worked very well for me, both for domestic and international shipments, as it saves on the cost of shipping a box. Of course, use my idea with common sense. If you are shipping something fragile, bulky or heavy, you will need to use a box. If you are shipping internationally, again, use this method with discretion.

Other Miscellaneous Packing Supplies

I purchase all my other miscellaneous packing supplies, like packing tape, from Staples at low cost. I will discuss how I save money on supplies in the Staples section.

5 Starting Out -- Selling Your Old Stuff

OK, so you now know the ins-and-outs of eBay shipping. But what do you sell on eBay? eBay's roots are in online garage-sale like auctions. Many people start by selling old, unwanted things around their house.

eBay will allow you to sell almost anything except prohibited items including: live animals, Nazi memorabilia, human remains and parts, and goods from embargoed countries like Cuba. The full list of restricted and prohibited items can be found at (http://ebay.to/1ybHc03).

These are items around your house that you can consider selling on eBay: used books, DVDs, CDs, old clothes, appliances (for parts if they are no longer in working condition), branded shoes that are still in good condition and tools. Selling these items will give you a good start and get your feet wet with little to no-risk.

While you might be able to clear some clutter and put some money back in your pocket, selling your old items is not a sustainable business plan. Do not expect everything you list on eBay to sell. Remember: you can also try listing these items on Craigslist, or Facebook local garage sales sites etc. If all else fails, you can donate your items.

Some eBay books will tell you that everything sells eventually. I have to disagree with that. Some things are simply destined for the dumpster. Do not expect someone to buy a piece of useless crap just because you listed it on eBay!

Do not be disheartened if you are not very successful in selling your cast-offs on eBay. Consider it practice in learning about how eBay works, keeping up with customer service and how to ship items. You will build some experience and feedback while selling old items

At the time of writing, eBay allows you to list up to 50 items per month for free. Try to take advantage of the full 50 item per month allotment if you can. If that is not possible, **aim to have at least 20 items listed on eBay at any one time.**

I have learned from past experience that if I have less than 20 items listed at any one time, the number of sales I make tends to tank. My guess is that if you only have 1 or 2 items listed on eBay, the chances of someone finding and buying your item reduces drastically.

On the other hand, if someone finds one of your listings and instead of clicking away because you did not have anything else to sell, the prospective buyer may instead find something else to buy from those 20 items you have listed. You can streamline the listing process by downloading eBay's free, Tubolister program at http://ebay.to/NO7iVr.

6 FINDING ITEMS TO SELL

To Purchase or Not to Purchase Wholesale?

Some eBay guidebooks may say that eBay is a volume business. I'll have to respectfully disagree. In my chapter on shipping, I showed how you can easily, unexpectedly lose money even when it looks like you are making a profit. Volume means nothing if you are losing money. Dealing in volume or wholesale purchasing can be very risky, especially if you are starting out.

Reselling items you purchased wholesale may have worked in eBay's earlier years but these days, you will often find wholesalers themselves selling on eBay. If you have a big stock of items in hand, you have to make sure you can sell it fast enough, and that your market is big enough to support you, and all your other competitors.

The market constantly changes. What sells today may not sell tomorrow. Worse, you may be squeezed out of the market by other sellers. In 2002, I wanted to expand my eBay business and supply. So I, together with my mother, headed to the Canton Import Export Fair in China (http://cantonfair.org.cn/en/). It is a very large fair where manufacturers from all over China, and buyers from all over the world, descend to trade.

We spent days at the fair and brought home many samples (teas, figurines, clothing, housewares, disposable tableware etc) and manufacturer contacts. Amongst the samples I listed on eBay to test the market were three life-sized decorative animals: two kittens and one dog. All sold quickly with a good profit margin. I proceeded to place a minimum amount wholesale order with the China-based manufacturer - $3000. I wired the funds to the factory and held my breath - I did not know if I would be scammed or not.

All went well and the order arrived in decent time as promised. Stock stacked high in my parent's apartment, I happily listed more of these decorative animals on eBay. Nothing sold. Zip zilch zero. I was stuck with that stock. My mother has since given the lot away. I am not sure to whom but I am glad to be rid of them.

I have not dealt in wholesale purchasing since, nor do I plan to do so in the future. Again, this is based on my personal experience and risk tolerance. Purchasing your supply on a wholesale level may work for you. Just because it did not work for me does not mean it will not work for you, and vice versa. *The market often shifts.*

If you'd like to try your hand at selling items purchased at wholesale from China, here are some websites you can start off with:
http://www.alibaba.com
http://dhgate.com
http://www.made-in-china.com

Selling Storage Auction or Garage/Estate Sale Finds

What about storage auctions or garage sales? Many sellers like to prowl storage auctions or garage/estate sales for items to list on eBay. Yes, you can certainly make money on your finds - if you find the right items to sell for the right price and hit the right market. In fact, you can possibly score big and make a lot of money on some finds.

Personally, I am not a fan of selling garage sale finds. The risk is high - you may be stuck with a bunch of useless, ugly crap destined only for your own garage sale. The fact is, these days, unless the garage sale seller was incapable of trying to sell their stuff on eBay first, most things you find are things that the seller wasn't able to sell on eBay, and are simply getting rid of them at the garage sale.

Exceptions are storage auctions or estate sales where everything is being sold at once in one place. Hitting up garage sales held by older people offer better potentials for good finds.

Disadvantages of Garage Sales/Storage Auctions

There are a few reasons why I do not like looking for garage sale items to sell on eBay. Firstly, garage sale items are almost always used, without packaging or in questionable condition. Garage sale items need extra care: cleaning, examination, a lot of description about the condition, any damage the item may have, and lots of photos to show the item in every direction.

Often, all that work goes into a one-time listing which may or may not sell. By one-time listing, I mean that you cannot apply the description or photos to similar items you may be selling.

Secondly, doing your pre-purchase research is harder. Checking completed listings for the "old german beer stein" you scored will probably yield a lot of "old german beer steins" that look nothing like the one you found.

Thirdly, the market for garage sale finds may be limited. It may also be dependant on the condition of the item. The completed listing that sold for a lot of money and got you excited with your exact same find, may have been in better condition and therefore worth money, whereas the item you found in poor condition may not be worth anything.

The fourth problem is pricing problems. If your completed search on Google yields nothing, how much do you possibly price your finds at?

Finally, scouring storage auctions or garage/estate sales is hard work. You have to spend time, effort and gas to all these garage sales which may or may not yield anything. If attending garage sales is a hobby of yours anyway, you know what you're doing and you want to try your hand at eBaying some of your finds, go for it.

But if you're hoping to find a big score for eBay, you might be disappointed. I feel that this last point is not mentioned in many other How-to eBay books. Authors of eBay books that write about how much profits they made from their garage sale excursions can be deceptive.

The reasons I have provided are not to say never go to garage or estate sales in hopes of finding goods to sell.

Many people do find good things to resell and are able to make good money from it.

However, that is also dependant on the quality of your local garage sales. I will reiterate that I do not think garage/estate sales should be where you get most of your eBay inventory. I think it fine as a small or side niche, but to me, the work and risk is too great for it to work as your mainstay eBay offering.

Items to Look Out for at Garage/Estate Sales

Items that I suggest looking out for at garage/estate sales include antiques, vintage items, old toys, retro toys (eg toys from the 1980s and 1990s), and artwork (if you know what you are looking for).

Researching Items and Prices

Nowadays, with smartphones, you can lower your risk by first checking if the items you find have any value on eBay before making the purchase. eBay's free app (http://mobile.ebay.com/) will help you while you are out and about.

To see if something sells, simply type in the item you've found and search under "Completed Listings". To find the "Completed Listings" section, go to the word "Advanced' next to the eBay search box on top of the page. Click on the "Advanced" button, enter your search term, scroll down and check the box "Completed Listings".

Search "Completed Listings" over "Sold Listings". Completed listings will give you a better idea of the proportion of similar items sold as compared to the number of listings unsold. This gives you an idea of market demand.

Do not search current listings. Just because someone has listed that exact same vase you have found for $10,000 does not mean that they are going to be able to sell it for $10,000, or even $5 for that matter.

Some sellers also use a subscription-based service called Terapeak (http://www.terapeak.com/) which offers additional eBay and Amazon Completed Listing data. I have not personally used this service but it may be of interest to some readers. Other websites that you may find helpful include:
http://www.watchcount.com
http://popular.ebay.com
http://www.whatsellsbest.com

Even though completed listings are a good indicator of demand and sale price, just like the stock market, past performance is not an indicator of future performance. Someone might have been able to sell that little vase for $10,000 but that does not mean that you will be able to sell it for that price. In fact, that one buyer who bought it for $10,000 might be the one and only buyer for that item. Period.

In addition to closing price for the items you are looking at, you should also see how many of these items have sold in the past. The more completed listings that you see in green, the higher the likelihood that there is a healthy market for your item, ie; there is a good chance you will have a buyer for your item.

7 Fixed Price or Auction-Style?

If you found something that you don't know what to price it at, I suggest using eBay's auction-style listing. In the auction-style, you can set your starting bid, then have your auction run for 1, 3, 5, 7 or 10 days. People are allowed to place their bid during this period and at the end of the listing duration, the item goes to the highest bidder.

In the early days, eBay was an online auction-only website. Meaning, everything listed on eBay had to be sold auction-style. You could list something starting at a $0.99 bid and the listing could potentially end at hundreds of dollars. It was a great way to buy and sell all the fun collectibles and rare finds back in the day. It certainly was exciting to watch your auction listings climb in bids, especially at the last minute.

According to eBay's current policy, the winning bidder has 2 days to pay up before the seller can open an unpaid item complaint. Filing the complaint will allow you, as the seller, to do one of two things. It will either remind the buyer to pay up, and if he does, you can complete the sale, or if he doesn't, there will be a strike against the buyer's account.

You will be allowed to cancel the sale and relist the item, and eBay will refund you the commission that you were charged for the transaction that was not completed. You will need to go to http://resolutioncenter.ebay.com/ to file a complaint.

If you have a garage/estate sale item and you are not sure what its value is, you should consider listing it auction-style.

You can choose to start the listing at $0.99 ala old-school eBay and try your luck. However, these days, those $0.99 or $0.01 starting bids are not as effective as they once were in getting bidder attention.

I suggest pricing your starting bid at double what you paid for your item. This will cover the cost of your item, eBay and paypal fees (which will run you about 15% of the total sale including shipping charges) and give you a small profit.

If it sells, excellent! If not, you can try relisting it again using the auction-style format, or using the fixed-price format at your starting bid (you may want to try listing it fixed-price at a slightly higher price than your initial auction starting bid). If it continues to not sell, you might have to lower your price. You may sometimes have to take a loss to clear your stock.

These days, with so many people selling on eBay, and with the economy as it currently is, auction bid prices do not rise like they used to. Most items are listed at fixed-price. Meaning you just set the price you want to sell your item at. In addition to the durations listed earlier, you can set fixed price listings to run for 30 days (meaning the listing will end when there is a sale or until the 30 days are up), or you can run your listing "Good Till Canceled", meaning the listing will run indefinitely until it sells or until you end it manually.

I have listed many items this way. Some have sold within a day. Others took *years* before finally selling, while still others have not sold to this day.

The nice thing about fixed-priced listings is that you can require "immediate payment" (check the box under your listing price when you list your item). "Immediate payment required" means the buyer has to pay immediately via paypal before he can close the listing and finalize the deal. You do not run the risk of having to deal with a non-paying buyer because payment is received immediately and you can just ship your order out.

8 STACKING DEALS

Remember when I mentioned **buy low and sell high**? Many books will talk about buying low and selling high, but I am going to take it a step further and give you some additional tricks on how to pad your profit margins.

Padding Profits with Credit Cards

Disclaimer: I am not a financial professional. Anything I discuss is based on my own experience and how that has helped me to pad my earning from eBay sales. If you need financial advice or any other kind of advice like tax or credit advice etc, please seek the appropriate professional for help. Anything I say is for informational purposes only.

There are many credit cards in the market today. The main purveyors are Visa, Mastercard, American Express (Amex) and Discover. Many credit cards will offer some kind of rewards program. If you have a credit card that does not reward you, I suggest looking into applying for a card that will give your rewards (note: applying for a credit card or for too many cards may lower your credit score).

Credit cards usually offer rewards in the form of a percentage cash back on your purchases, or air miles. I personally prefer American Express which gives you extra protections like extended warranty, easy purchase disputes and cash back rewards.

If you have certain American Express cards, you might also be eligible for special or targeted offers that they may be running at that time. Deals have included statement credits for making certain dollar amounts at specified retailers like Walmart or Staples.

I cannot say which card offers the best rewards as it really seems to be dependant on what American Express decides to promote at one time. Promotions may also be user targeted.

If you do not want to sign up for a credit card, you can also get a reloadable pre-paid card from American Express called Serve (http://srve.co/1ArNmfK) which will allow you to take advantage of many American Express deals. They will, however, charge a $1 monthly service fee unless you live in New York, Texas and Vermont.

If you already have an American Express card, be sure to sign up for their social network-exclusive offers:

Amex Facebook Sync: http://bit.ly/1wacnWr
Amex Twitter Sync: http://amex.co/1busTtl
Amex Foursquare Sync: http://amex.co/1Cg4VS8
Amex TripAdvisor Sync: http://amex.co/1xzBbhg

Amex Sync offers usually consist of statement credit deals. For example, spend at least $100 at Best Buy, receive a $25 statement credit and so forth.

American Express seems to be the most aggressive in their promotional deals. However, in the past few years, Mastercard also seems to have been trying to elbow their way into the offer arena. Offers normally are most prevalent during the Black Friday - Christmas period. However, deals do pop up year round. I suggest following these companies on social media like Facebook or Twitter to keep up with any ongoing promotions.

Of course, make sure you use your credit cards responsibly. You may be hit with high interest charges if your balance is not paid in full before the end of the grace period. To maximise your profits, you must make sure you do not end up paying these or any other additional fees which can quickly kill your profit.

Debit Cards Can Help As Well

If you are not comfortable with credit cards, you can also consider using a debit card to help boost your bottom line a little more. Some debit cards, including the Paypal debit card, will offer you cash back on all your purchases made on the card. You can order a Paypal debit card for free via Paypal.

To order a debit card from Paypal, log in to your Paypal account. There is a submenu under the "My Account". Under "Withdraw", another submenu will reveal a tab which says "Paypal Debit Mastercard". The button will take you to the link where you can apply for your card. The card will be linked to your Paypal funds and will draw from your Paypal account. You should receive your card in the mail in about a week or so after your application is approved.

Paypal debit currently offers 1% cash-back on all your purchases. However, using the Paypal debit does not automatically mean that you get the 1% cash-back. You will need to sign up for the program before the cash-back will apply.

To sign up:

- Log into your Paypal Account
- Click on the **Profile** button on the top menu.
- Click **My Money**.
- Click **Update** (next to the "Paypal Debit Mastercard Business Card Summary")
- Click **Enroll**.

You will then be enrolled in the cash-back program.

The downside to debit cards is that you do not get the same level of purchase protection that credit cards afford you.

Using Gift Cards to Your Benefit

Having not grown up in the US, I have never really gotten the point of store gift cards. To me, it seems like a scam that stores use to trick you into giving them money that you may never end up spending at their store.

However, there are a couple of ways that you can utilize gift cards to pad your profits. Firstly, you can purchase gift cards at below store value at certain places. Companies where you can buy gift cards at below face value include Cardpool.com, Cardcash.com, Raise.com and of course, on eBay. Shop around. The different sites offer different discount rates for respective retailer gift cards.

Companies like Cardpool.com verify the gift card amount (from the card number) before reselling it. However, there is a risk that the original seller of the unwanted gift card can copy the number and syphon the value of the funds on the card once they have received payment for the gift card by cardpool. I have never personally encountered this problem but I have read about it.

All three sites offer some kind of buyer protection. I would also use my trusty credit card both to protect my purchase, as well as to stack discounts. Here's how a current real-world example works: You purchased a $25 Best Buy gift card for $24.12. You used your credit/debit card which gives you 1% back on your purchases (some cards may give you even more cash-back but 1% is the norm).

So your credit/debit card gives you a cash-back of $0.24 for the $24.12 purchase. So your actual final price for the Best Buy gift card is now $23.88. You have now lowered your expense by 4.48% on a $25 Best Buy purchase - less cost = more profit.

Finally, there is TwoSmiles by HP (https://www.twosmiles.com/). TwoSmiles offers print-at-home gift cards. From time to time, they offer excellent promotional coupon codes like 20% off gift cards from select retailers.

At the time of writing, TwoSmiles was offering 20% off gift cards from Old Navy, Bass Pro Shops, Forever 21, The Gap,

Banana Republic, Sports Authority and Aeropostale. Taking advantage of discounts such as these will help to boost your profit margins tremendously if you are already sourcing for products at these retailers.

Maximizing Profits - Save On Gas with Gift Cards

Another unlikely way to stack deals by way of gift card purchases is at certain grocery store chains. In Colorado, the two main grocery store chains that offer gift card deals are King Soopers (part of the Kroger chain), and Safeway (which includes Vons, Pavilions, Tom Thumb and Randall's).

Both companies give you gas points when you make purchases with your Club membership (memberships are free). In general, you will get 1 gas point per dollar spent on most items (certain purchases such as tobacco, gas, and lottery do not qualify).

When you reach 100 points, you get $0.10 off a gallon of gas at participating gas stations (up to $1 off/per gallon and up to 25 gallons at Safeway, or up to 35 gallons per redemption at Kroger). Points expire the last day of the month after you earn the points (ie: if you earned the points in June, they will expire on July 31st).

When you buy gift cards, however, their current every-day point reward is 2 gas points per dollar spent on store gift cards. That is, you accumulate $0.10 off a gallon for every $50 you spend on gift cards. Both stores also often run bonus gift card promotions - 4x gas points - where you earn $0.10 off per gallon for every $25 spent on gift cards.

If you maximize points up to the $1 discount, and fill an empty tank, your savings will be as much as $25 at Safeway, and $35 at Kroger. If you have a smaller gas tank, you should consider bringing a gas can to take full advantage of the savings.

You can redeem Kroger gas points at Kroger gas stations or participating Shell stations. You can redeem your Safeway gas points at Safeway gas stations or participating Chevron, Texaco, Exxon and Mobil gas stations (http://bit.ly/1rcMeny).

Maximizing Profits - Saving with Grocery Store Deals

In addition to accumulating gas points, you can potentially pad your profits by signing up for Kroger's and/or Safeway's digital coupon programs:

Kroger: http://bit.ly/1uPhvUQ
Safeway: http://bit.ly/1jBk8EO

I do not shop at Kroger much so I will focus mainly on how you can maximize profits through Safeway. It may be worth your while to sign up for Safeway's Just4U program. There are two coupon categories in the link above. The "Coupon Center" is where you get coupons that apply to everyone who has signed up for Just4U.

"Personalized Deals" that you can load onto your Club card. They are targeted digital coupons that Safeway generates based on your purchase history. Safeway digital coupons are normally updated every Wednesday. However, I have seen coupons appear on other days so it is best to check your Just4U account before heading to the store. You have to click the "Add" button before discounts are applied at checkout. You also have to enter your Club card information before the discounts come off at the register.

Throughout the year, Safeway may issue deals which can include 4x gas points, $10 off $50 a store gift card (promotions vary but I have seen deals like the $10 off a $50 GAP gift card purchase), $0.40-$0.80 off per gallon of gas when you spend $30-$80 (again, targeted promotions vary), as well as discounts off prepaid American Express/Visa/Mastercard cards.

For example, they may offer $10 off a purchase of a $100 American Express prepaid card. There is usually a load fee of around $5.96 for these prepaid cards so with the discount offer, you will normally end up with a 4-5% "profit". Use your prepaid card to buy store gift cards to accumulate more gas points.

Finally, their Catalina deals. Catalina coupons are coupons that print out at the checkstand when you checkout. Safeway often conducts offers similar to the prepaid card or gift card purchase deals that you might get on Just4U. However, instead of an instant discount off your purchase, you will (usually,) get a $10 off your next purchase coupon that will print out on the Catalina.

You can often find Catalina gift card deals before special occasions like Mother's Day, Father's Day and Graduation. Catalina prepaid card deals are normally offered at the start of the new season: Fall, Spring, Summer and Winter.

Catalina offers are not usually limited and you can buy as many prepaid cards as you like (make separate purchase transactions). However, these offers are not as attractive since it requires an additional purchase.

There will also be quite a number of deals offered in various combinations during the pre-Christmas period. There are often deals on iTunes giftcards before Christmas. Unlike most other gift cards, you can sell iTunes gift cards on eBay at or around 10% above face value. Your customers will almost definitely be foreign.

Why? I believe it is because foreign buyers need US iTunes gift cards to access the US iTunes offerings. In 2012, many of the deals overlapped, discounting some gift cards to as much as 20-30% off. However, in 2013, Safeway must have gotten wiser as there were fewer overlapping deals.

Albertsons also conducts similar dollar-off coupon deals with a minimum gift card purchase. Unfortunately, I do not patronize Albertsons enough to discuss their deals in detail. With Albertson's purchase of Safeway stores, deals at both chains may be synchronized.

I like to keep Amazon, Best Buy, Kohls, Staples and Target gift cards on hand. Other gift cards that can be useful are Home Depot, Lowes, GameStop, Sears, Macy's and Toys R Us. Of course, always stack your deals by using your cash-back credit/debit card.

9 Finding *NEW* Items to Sell

Many eBay books will tell you to find a niche that you can specialize in. I agree to a certain extent. You should try to find a niche for your eBay business. However, I do not think that you should pigeonhole yourself to any one niche. Why do I say this?

As I mentioned in the beginning of this book, things constantly change. By that, I mean trends, fads, eBay policies, technologies, economies, laws etc which can change over time and which can affect your eBay niche.

Here are some examples of the niches that have risen and fallen for me since 1998:

- Anime videos and other memorabilia lasted ~ 3 years
- Movie magazines/postcards/TV guides/celebrity article clipping lots lasted ~ 5 years
- Britney Spears/Backstreet Boys (remember them?) memorabilia lasted as long as they were popular
- HD-DVDs lasted until they became redundant
- Custom signs and banners lasted ~4 years - This business followed the business and real estate boom (real estate signs + all kinds of small business signs) and bust (foreclosure and pawn store signs). The market eventually became too saturated to sustain us.

- New movie DVD releases lasted ~3 years (I doubled my money on the new release DVDs that I invested in by reselling them to Australians. They were happy to pay for movies on DVDs which were just being released in theatres in Australia).
- Chumbys (google it). This was an item that only had an international audience as it was initially only available in the US. My niche ride lasted about 6 months.

My list could go on, and on, but you get the picture.

10 ARBITRAGE AND THINKING LOCAL

When I say "think local" I do not mean garage sales etc. Think of your local large retailers. Some of these retailers are widespread only in certain regions. In fact, you probably see your local retailer so often that you don't even think of the things that are available freely to you, right under your nose!

However, their products garner interest outside their localities. Ikea is one example. In the Denver, Colorado area, we also have Costco and Trader Joe's. Perhaps you have Disneyland or Disneyworld at your doorstep. Perhaps you have Broadway, Hollywood, Las Vegas, London or simply a CVS drugstore close to where you live.

To figure out what to sell, you have to be an arbitrageur (a person who engages in arbitrage). What is arbitrage? Arbitrage, as defined on Wikipedia, is "the practice of taking advantage of a price difference between two or more markets: striking a combination of matching deals that capitalize upon the imbalance, the profit being the difference between the market prices."

Simply put: **buy low, sell high**. So what exactly does that mean and how does that help you to make money on eBay?

Markets are extremely inefficient. That gives you the opportunity to step into profit from the difference prices or scarcity in different markets. eBay levels the playing field for the individual or small-time seller by opening up markets which would otherwise not be easily accessible to you before.

I was able to make a lot of money this way in the early years by exporting Anime videos to the US from Singapore. It was easy to price items.

If I purchased something for S$50 (~US$28.50 at that time), I would start the bidding at US$50 which gave me an immediate profit of US$21.40 less eBay fees (Paypal did not charge processing fees in its early days). Of course, the higher the bids went, the more profit I made.

IMPORTANT :
NEVER MENTION THIS BOOK, OR THAT YOU ARE RESELLING YOUR PURCHASE ON EBAY/AMAZON.

Doing so will possibly ruin your source. Do not brag, be polite and keep a low profile. If you need to, say you stock up on Christmas presents when you see a deal.

Local Retailer Opportunities

Ikea

Similar to my Anime example, you can apply arbitrage even if you are in the US and only want to ship domestically. Let's say you live near an Ikea store. Ikea is a large Swedish furniture store with locations in select cities across the US (and worldwide). If you are not familiar with the store, then you probably do not have an Ikea near you. Think of it as Target meets Walmart meets Cost Plus World Market (if you have one in your region) for furniture. (See http://ikea.com/us/en for examples of what they sell.)

Ikea sells their furniture designs exclusively. You may find similarly inspired designs at other retailers but only Ikea sells Ikea furniture in the primary market. Ikea.com ships their items only on a very limited basis. Enter YOU: the secondary market. Your market is people who love Ikea's stuff but simply live too far away to shop there. It is possible for you to buy items from Ikea (even at retail price), resell it for a higher price and make a profit. If you are able to pounce on their clearance items or discontinued designs, your may increase your profit margins further.

In this particular example, reselling Ikea's products offers you an additional perk: they design everything to be packed as flat as possible, to be assembled by the buyer. That means that almost everything you buy from there is already pre-packed into a neat box, ready to be shipped out!

Since Ikea's 2011 opening in Colorado, I was able to resell quite a number of Ikea items which I had purchased at *retail pricing.*

I even had a customer contact me about helping her do some personal Ikea shopping and then having all the items shipped to her in another state. We agreed on a mark up for my gas, time and effort and everyone was happy!

Unfortunately, Ikea is almost an hour away from where I live, so while it is a potential eBay source for people who live closer to a store, it is not very cost effective for me to make Ikea more than an occasional supplier.

Be sure to sign up for Ikea's free IKEA FAMILY membership (http://bit.ly/Z7sdbl) which gives you FAMILY discounts and free coffee or tea at their resturant.

Items I Look Out for at IKEA

Anything. IKEA sells its own designs almost exclusively. I personally prefer to stick with the smaller, easy to ship items but anything is a potential resalable item at IKEA.

Trader Joe's

People *love* Trader Joe's. For those of you reading this book who have a Trader Joe's near you, you probably know "Joe". For those of you who do not, Trader Joe's is this hip grocery store with funky decor, unusual food products and helpful employees.

Like Ikea, they sell unusual products not quite found anywhere else including: Cookie Butter (yes it is ground up cookies), Chocolate Covered Potato Chips and Chocolate Covered Banana Bites.

Here is an example of how you can sell products pretty risk-free with a little bit of effort. With your smartphone, you can easily snap photos of their product to list on eBay. You can use the eBay app to do this easily (http://bit.ly/1oUz7cb or http://mobile.ebay.com/). The risk however, is the product you might have pre-sold on eBay gets sold out when you come back for it.

If you are selling something before you have it in hand, be sure to abide by eBay's pre-sale policy (http://ebay.to/1ra16Kk). If you do not feel comfortable selling in this manner, you can always buy some of the products and then list it for sale.

Choose items that you won't mind keeping for yourself. That way, if it doesn't sell, you can consumer it! While this suggestion is not necessarily the way to run your eBay business, in this particular instance, the products are cheap and consumable and I think the low cost outweighs any "risk" of your product not selling.

Items I Look Out for at Trader Joe's

Items I look out for would be unusual food items that are exclusive to Trader Joe's. Pay particular attention to items with purchase limits.

Wholesale Clubs

Costco

I have made a lot of money reselling Costco merchandise over the years. We were unimpressed with costs when we first visited the store. Sure, they had a lot big jugs and containers of pickles and mayonnaise, but we were not convinced that the membership was worth the bulk savings.

While I still think Costco is not the final stop for deals, it is a good place for decent everyday prices on their varied selection of quality products. Like Trader Joe's, Costco carries a wide range of good quality products co-branded under their Kirkland Signature line.

Additionally, many things including designer brands like Lucky Jeans and Calvin Klein clothing are frequently sold at a fraction of retail prices. Costco changes their stock frequently so if you see something that's a good deal, jump on it! It may not be there the next time you are at the store. I am still beating myself up for only picking up two Pixar blu-ray gift sets that were marked down to $9.99 each!

Couponing at Costco

Costco sends out a monthly coupon book which gives you additional dollar savings on top of their regular prices. In the past, you would need to tear out the coupons and present them at check-out but it looks like Costco is moving towards just automatically deducting the applicable coupon amount(s) from your purchases at checkout.

The company does not accept manufacturer coupons. If you purchased something the month prior without coupon, you should be able to price adjust your item when the new coupon is released.

Again, I am not sure if this is a corporate procedure or if it varies by store. Regardless, if the service desk refuses, you can always ask if you can rebuy the item while the coupon is in effect and return that same item using your old receipt.

Costco Memberships

Gold Star (personal) and Business Memberships are currently $55 per year. It would be better to sign up for a Business Membership for your eBay business. With Business, you can purchase products for personal, business and resale use. You will need to provide Costco with your resale license to purchase items tax-free for resale.

Different states have different rules on how you need to process items for resale. Check with your local authorities, as well as your local Costco. I have found that different retailers, even within the same state, have different procedures for waiving sales tax on resale items.

As you start to expand, you can consider the Executive Membership which is currently $110 per year but gives you 2% back on all your purchases (up to $750 per year). Your cash back comes in a form of a Costco check which you use to purchase more products. I am not sure if this applies to all branches, but in the past, if I did not spend the full check amount, my local Costco just returned the unused balance of the check in the form of cash.

The nice thing about Executive Membership is that if you did not recoup the extra $55 you paid in the form of rebates, you can ask the membership desk for a refund. Again, check with your local branch. I am not sure if this is standard corporate protocol, or if it varies by location.

Finally, a secret way to shop at Costco without having to pay the annual membership fee is to have someone else who does have a membership buy Costco gift cards for you.

Costco will allow you to shop there without a membership if you have a gift card. An alternative would be to purchase a membership, then purchase enough gift cards for your purchases for the next year, when your membership expires.

If you are not happy with your membership, Costco will refund you your dues at any time. However, I do not recommend that you abuse this unless you really do not like shopping there.

Occasionally, daily deal sites like Groupon (http://bit.ly/1GW4ydo)* and LivingSocial (http://bit.ly/13EEbMO)* have offered Costco (and Sam's Club) membership discounts. Deals have in the past only applied for new memberships and not to membership renewals. However, I have been able to apply the discounts to my renewals. Your success rate may vary.

Costco/American Express Credit Card

You can also choose to sign up for the American Express TrueEarnings Card. The annual fee is waived with your Costco membership dues. The credit card currently gives you an additional 1% cash back on all Costco purchases as well as 3% cash back at all gas stations. On this note, I will also add that American Express is the only credit card that Costco accepts. You can use cash or checks but they do not accept Visa, Mastercard or Discover. I have never had a TrueEarnings Card. I think that there are other cards out there with better rewards options.

Additional Costco Tips

Here are some additional Costco tips according to Lifehacker (http://bit.ly/1c0MC5p):

- *"Prices that end in 97¢: These have been marked down from the regular priced items, which end in 99¢.*
- *Odd pricing, such as 79¢, 49¢, or 89¢: These indicate specially priced items that Costco got a deal from the manufacturer. Rapoport says these can be better deals than at other stores, but not usually better than the 97¢ markdown.*
- *An asterisk* on the upper right side of the sign: The item won't be reordered.*
- *88¢ or .00 endings: Manager markdowns. Sometimes the company uses these to move a product very fast."*

Items I Look Out for at Costco

Items I look out for include clearance items, branded clothing and Kirkland Signature Brand shelf-stable food items.

Sam's Club

Sam's Club is a wholesale club owned by Walmart. In my view, it is Costco's poorer cousin. Think of it like Walmart except in bulk. I have held memberships at both Sam's and Costco for quite a number of years now and in my view, Costco beats Sam's hands down. If you are on a budget and trying to decide on which Club to join, I suggest joining Costco.

Sam's Club Membership

Sam's Club's regular membership costs $45 annually while their Plus membership is $100 annually. In return for the Plus membership, you get extra coupon savings on certain products at Sam's throughout the year.

Additionally, Plus Members now get $10 for every $500 spent on qualifying purchases, which is roughly equivalent to Costco's Executive Membership 2% back perk. You can earn up to $500 back in rewards per 12 month period.

I have never been a Plus member since I do not feel like I can get really good deals from Sam's for resale, or for my personal consumption in general. Again, Sam's Club has run membership discounts via LivingSocial which made it worthwhile for me to rejoin the Club.

Deals at Sam's

Be sure to check out Sam's clearance section (it is usually tucked in one of the corners of the store). I have also found good clearance deals at Sam's after the Christmas season. Deals I have scored in bulk for resale include gourmet chocolate and Aerogardens (when they were in vogue).

Clearance prices vary by store location. If an item is eligible for "Click 'n' Pull" (basically store pickup) service, you check prices based on store location at samsclub.com. To check prices, select the product you are looking at then change the store location(s). The price may vary, especially if the item is on clearance. If you use the "Click 'n' Pull" service, you will have to pick up your order at that specific store.

Items I Look Out for at Sam's

I do not feel that Sam's is a very good source for eBay resellers. I look out for clearance items.

Costco, Ikea, Sam's Club and Trader Joe's are just some examples of local stores that you can use as product sources to your advantage by harnessing arbitrage. The point of this chapter is so that you open yourself up to these local source opportunities.

Other sources that I had heard other sellers use to their local advantage include Disney and CVS. I cannot go into detail with these sources as I do not have direct experience with them. However, I was told that there are many resale opportunities for their commonly occurring close-out sales.

What if you do not have access to any big regional retail sources? How about thinking about what your state or area is well known for?

For example, Utah is big in honey. Perhaps you can get your hands on a cheap, good-quality source - that may be something to look into. It is impossible for me to know what you can get locally so my intention is for you to keep your mind open to any and all possibilities.

11 FREE IS GOOD

In the late 1990s and early 2000s, promotional postcards were all the rage as a new form of advertising in many countries. They were usually distributed on racks at stores, cinemas and coffeehouses. This advertising and distribution format seemed to be very popular in most major cities outside the US during this time.

These cards advertised anything from new movie releases (which were very popular on eBay at that time) to cars, to alcohol and perfume. The postcards were free for the taking and were very prevalent in Singapore at that time.

Selling these free postcards on eBay made up the bulk of my business for almost five years. This was a fun time during my eBay selling career. I had just graduated and even though the dot-com boom had already crashed, there seemed to be a worldwide audience and market for these little freebies.

Collecting and selling these free postcards either paid for, or subsidized my travels to many countries. Places I found postcards to sell included (of course) Singapore, Thailand, Germany, the UK, Canada, the Netherlands, Hong Kong and Japan (they give out promotional flyers called *Chirashi* instead of postcards).

What does my story have to do with you? It has a lot to do with you if you live in a city like Las Vegas, Manhattan or London. Cities which host a lot of tourists and/or conventions provide a lot of freebie opportunities for possible resale on eBay. You simply have to look at everything as an eBay seller and not as the general public. Anything related to shows, musicals, music bands, performances, celebrities, video games, sporting events (especially big ones), niche conventions can have a potential resale market on eBay.

I mentioned the above three cities because cities such as these tend to hand out more free promotional material that can possibly be resold available.

The San Diego Comic Con (SDCC)

If you live in San Diego or its surrounding areas, you should know about the SDCC. The SDCC is by far the source of the biggest motherload of resalable items (both free and otherwise) that I have found. Before we had kids, my husband, my mother and I would make an annual 17-plus hour drive to the SDCC.

After all trip expenses (including gas, exorbitant hotel rates, enjoying the San Diego food scene etc), we would always still come out with at least a $5000 profit. We would normally net about $3000 in profits within a month from the end of the SDCC.

The SDCC offers many opportunities for eBay resale including more freebies or "swag" than you can imagine, many SDCC-exclusive releases, limited-editions that are otherwise hard to find elsewhere, and celebrity and cast autograph opportunities. All of these items and events pose excellent opportunities for the eBay reseller.

It is a lot of fun but it is also a lot of work to collect, walk the exhibition halls, stand in line, organize all your SDCC "goodies", then to finally list and ship your items. If you are a serious SDCC eBay reseller, expect to work 12-15 hour days while the Convention is in session. Having 2 or more assistants to help you, and a truck to haul it all away will make a big difference in your SDCC efforts.

The success of the SDCC seems to be spawning Comic Cons across the country. While not affiliated with the SDCC, I have seen the Denver Comic Con grow each year since its inception in 2012. These new Comic Cons hold potential eBay reseller opportunities for eBay sellers across the country in the future.

Items I Look Out for at the SDCC

Good items to keep an eye out for at the SDCC include all free and promotional items from toy companies, movie studios and video game companies. Any free items that feature popular themes, for example the books and/or movie "Twilight", comic book heroes (think Batman, Spider-Man etc), zombies or whatever is popular at the time you are reading this book. Remember - Free is Good.

Getting your hands on cast autographs is an excellent idea. These events are usually free but require time and planning to get in the autograph line. When we attended the SDCC, shows like "Heroes", "Chuck" and "The Big Bang Theory" were popular shows. Autographed and exclusive items featuring these shows were all very profitable.

SDCC exclusives from urban vinyls to movie memorabilia to video game memorabilia are all good potential resale items. Other good possibilities include anything that is double-themed.

For example, Lego Batman. These may not be free but anything that has crossed over from books to movies, or video games to movies and toys etc, are also particularly good resale candidates.

The best time to list all your SDCC items is during and within a month after the Convention ends. After which, sales and prices will start to decline.

12 FINDING ITEMS FOR RESALE FROM RETAILERS

As I mentioned in earlier chapters, things on eBay have changed quite a bit since its early days. Instead of people paying premium prices for hard-to-find items, eBay has now become the to-go place to purchase new items at below retail pricing.

How then, can you sell new items without having to go the wholesale route? My answer is to get deals from clearance sales, by stacking deals, and/or by purchasing store exclusives.

I. Best Buy

When my niche evolved into selling DVDs, Best Buy and the now defunct Circuit City were *the* place for me to purchase my eBay stock. Best Buy seems to pride itself in offering all kinds of store-exclusives with its DVD and later, video game releases. Back then, I would check http://forum.dvdtalk.com/ often to keep up on the DVD releases.

Best Buy would often release special and exclusive packaging as well as Best Buy exclusive promotional items (these would range anywhere from plush toys to pens to notebooks, just to name a few).

I shipped these purchased-at-retail price DVDs overseas, mainly to Australia, where Australians were willing to pay twice what I had paid at retail for original-release DVDs to movies that were just being shown in Australian theatres. Sometimes, these movies had not yet been released in Australia!

In the meantime, I would sell the store exclusives which were usually limited in run to others who had not been able to get their hands on said exclusive in time. Almost every Tuesday, my husband will make as many as 10 store stops to purchase exclusives.

Unfortunately, the interest in DVDs died down as the economy sunk then crashed in 2008. To add to the DVD's death knell, now redundant HD-DVDs and blu-rays were starting to take off as the new media.

At this time, I started noticing "CAG" appearing on dvdtalk.com. "CAG" is an acronym for cheapassgamer.com. It is the video game equivalent to dvdtalk.com. I also started reading news articles about the success of GameStop and how electronic retailers like Best Buy wanted a piece of the growing gaming pie.

At the store level, the dvd selection shrunk while the video game section started becoming bigger and more dedicated. By this time, Circuit City had shut its doors for good. I decided to follow the leader. I replicated my dvd reselling tactics to reselling video games with great success.

In its same form, Best Buy started releasing store-exclusives. Some exclusives were physical releases which ranged from coasters to figures. Like GameStop, they also had Best Buy-exclusive digital download codes which could consist of special characters, powers, weapons or outfits.

Often, the store will give you a special download code for pre-ordering a game. Rare pre-order download codes for popular games could sell for as much as or over $90!

Take-Home Tip: People will pay you for something they are unable to get. They may even *pay* you a premium price if supply is limited and demand is high.

Meanwhile, the Brazilians were buying up my video games. My profits were not as great as for my dvds but it was still a decent profit margin. What I did not know at that time was that Brazil was enjoying economic growth during one of America's most painful recessions. Would Brazilians have bought other merchandise? Possibly, but by keeping an eye on what was working and what was not, I had found a new niche and I ran with it.

Reward Zone Membership

To maximize profits at Best Buy, sign up for their free Reward Zone membership. You will get 1 point for every $1 spent. For every 250 points that you accumulate you will receive a $5 in Best Buy credit.

The credit comes in a printable store coupon. The more you spend at the store, the more rewards Best Buy grants on your membership. Visit http://bit.ly/1BHV2II for details.

Gamers Club Membership

If you want to delve into reselling video games you might want to consider joining the paid membership to Gamer's Club. Paid membership is currently priced at $119.99 for a two-year membership.

This membership gives you extra discounts off new games, bonus trade-in values for used games and exclusive game offers (which can give you very cheap or sometimes even free games). For more details, visit http://bit.ly/1xUD9sc.

If Best Buy becomes a big source for you, you might also want to consider signing up for their "My Best Buy" credit card which will earn you 5% back in rewards. I have never signed up for their card but it may be worth it for some. Visit http://bit.ly/Z7sTgX for more information.

Price-Matching at Best Buy

Best Buy will price match to local competitors as well as major online retailers like Amazon. Their return policy is below average (15 days with receipt and ID) but is extended for Elite and Elite Plus Reward Zone members.

Items I Look Out for at Best Buy

Best Buy's inventory is fairly electronic-specific. Items that I look out for at Best Buy are exclusive releases and clearanced items. You can check for your local store's clearanced and open-box pricing at http://tinyurl.com/qe7ovjy.

Maximizing Profits At Online Retailer Sources

Our weekly store runs decreased when Circuit City closed down and the economy slowed. Gas prices were soaring. I had my video game niche but I was also pregnant and it became increasingly difficult for me to travel all over the city to pick up merchandise.

My husband, while helpful during our buying trips, does not have the gumption to do any eBay purchasing without me. I turned to looking for deals online and found Slickdeals.net.

At first glance, it was a forum that did not seem like much. However, as I started to check the site often, it became my go-to place to find deals. It would also be my closely guarded secret until this book.

II. Slickdeals.net

According to Wikipedia, Slickdeals.net (SD) is a social forum site featuring crowdsourced deals and coupons from retailers such as Amazon (etc).

SD is one of the main forums where deal finders and seekers congregate and discuss deals from both online and brick and mortar stores. This is where you have to be open to all deals and almost all retailers.

NEVER MENTION SLICKDEALS, FATWALLET OR THIS BOOK AT ANY RETAILER.

If you are a new visitor to SD, you will need to familiarize yourself with common acronyms used:

- AC - After Coupon
- AR - After Rebate
- BB - Best Buy
- BM or B&M - Brick and Mortar storefront
- CAG - Cheapassgamer.com
- ER - Easy Rebate (usually refers to Staples Easy Rebate program. Details in the Staples section)
- FAR - Free After Rebate (these are usually good and usually apply to software)
- FS - Free Shipping
- FSS - Free Super Saver Shipping (applies to Amazon's free shipping for purchases totaling over $35)
- FW - FatWallet.com
- GC - (Best Buy's) Gamer's Club
- GC - Could also refer to gift card
- KC - Kohl's Cash
- KSO - (Amazon's) Kindle Special Offer
- MM - Money maker (meaning you can actually turn a profit on these deals, usually after you apply a coupon or rebate)
- OOP - Out Of Pocket (meaning the actual money you spent)
- OP - Original Poster (the person who started the thread)
- PM - Price Match
- PP - Paypal.com

- PP - Could also mean Photo Paper, depending on the context. You will see it appear in office supply store threads.
- RZ - (Best Buy's) Reward Zone
- SER - Staples Easy Rebate (details in the Staples section)
- S&H - Shipping and Handling
- YMMV - Your Mileage Will Vary (Meaning not all stores will have this deal and you may have to travel to a further store to replicate the deal.)

Each deal thread is rated by other users based on how easy it is to replicate the deal, price, and how reputable a merchant is. Frontpage deals are the best-rated deals. Frontpage deals, with a small fire icon, means that the deal is extra hot!

You will often see frontpage deals from Amazon.com, Best Buy, Staples, Kohl's, Newegg.com, Sears and Walmart. Good deals from these retailers normally will earn the "hot deal" trifecta.

Similar to eBay which brings customers to your listings 24/7, Slickdeals has deal finders on the forum 24/7, posting all kinds of good deals. "Slickdealers" are an awesome and helpful community.

If there is anything that you are not sure about in terms of realizing that awesome deal, be it questions about rebates or merchant reputation, someone is almost always there to help with advice, suggestions, or offer words of caution.

A downside to "Slickdealing" is that there are a lot of other eBay sellers also planning on reselling deals. What this means for you, as an eBay seller, is that eBay may now be flooded with the item you want to resell. Many resellers will list items on eBay once they have made the purchase (before the order arrives).

Personally, I will only list confirmed orders placed through Amazon Prime (the details are in the Amazon chapter). After the deal is posted on Slickdeals, and after you have made your purchase, you may start to see the going prices of your "slickdeal" plummeting on eBay.

How you react to eBay price drops will depend on your risk-tolerance and how liquid you need to stay. You may feel the need to drop your price to compete with others. However, I normally stick to my pricing based on Completed Listing prices prior to the market getting flooded, unless the product is a very short-lived item (like an electronic or software that is going to be discontinued or if an update is going to be released).

Otherwise, I suggest just waiting out the market with your item set at the price based on the *original* completed listing prices (before the market was temporarily saturated).

Since the market is highly imperfect, you will often find that someone ends up buying your item at the higher price, even though there are many other listings at lower prices. Other times, you may have to have the item listed for 2 or 3 months, maybe more, before the saturation tapers off and your item sells.

I have had items that languish for *years* on eBay before selling 5, sometimes 10, of these items within a month. Again, not everything sells. Sometimes, if you hold the item for too long, it never ends up selling. These items may be destined to end up at your garage sale or on Craigslist.

I suggest checking SlickDeals at least two, if not three times a day to keep updated on new sales or deals. Popular or limited-item sales sell out quickly once they are posted on the site. Think about something for too long and it might be gone!

Cashback Sites

If you find a good deal online, you can help to pad your profits/savings by purchasing the item through a cashback site. These sites are online retailer affiliates. They are paid a small commission, usually a percentage of a sale, for driving customers from their site to their affiliate's site.

The main cash-back sites I use are fatwallet.com, ebates.com and shopathome.com. In addition to being a cashback site, fatwallet.com also has a regularly updated crowdsourced deal forum similar to Slickdeals. I find it a little too much work to check more than one deal site so I just use Slickdeals for deal sourcing.

Other cashback sites include befrugal.com, bigcrumbs.com, mrrebates.com and extrabux.com. If you are collecting airline miles, many major airlines have similar cashback sections offering cash back in the form of air miles if you click through from their shopping partner cashback site.

Cashback offers vary depending on the site. Moreover, the cash back percentages are not static and can change, depending on the affiliate offer that one one cashback site may be running at that time. Fatwallet, for example, often runs double cashback deals for different stores at different times.

To maximize profits, I always check my three favorite cashback sites and click through from the site that is offering the highest cashback rates at that time. Keep in mind though, researching eBay to see if the Slickdeal is a resalable one, then checking the cashback sites for maximum returns, takes time and you will run the risk of the item selling out during the time you were doing your research!

III. Amazon.com

Believe it or not, you can get a lot of deals on Amazon to resell on eBay. Yes, you can buy deals on eBay to sell on Amazon as well but I will only discuss Amazon as a possible resale source.

Amazon is an online retail behemoth that many brick and mortar stores are now acknowledging. In the past, retailers like Best Buy and Staples would not price match against online stores (Amazon included).

I think the change in policy almost across the board of price-matching stores shows how much of a competitive threat Amazon is to other corporations. If you are reading this book, chances are you downloaded it from Amazon and are quite familiar with the corporation. I will not go into further detail as to the might that is: Amazon.

Amazon Price-Matching

Officially, Amazon does not price match, in that if you call Amazon and tell them you found another retailer selling an item for less, they will not price match. However, they do keep track of their major competitors' pricing and often automatically adjust their pricing to match those retailers.

The main stores that Amazon watches closely include what I call "the Big Three": Walmart, Best Buy and Target. To a lesser extent, they also monitor Newegg, Staples, Officemax/Office Depot and Sears/Kmart.

Additionally, you can tell Amazon "about a lower price". When you scroll to the bottom of each respective product page, after all the product reviews, there is a highlighted box which includes a link that allows you to "tell us about a lower price".

Product Details
File Size: 546 KB
Simultaneous Device Usage: Unlimited
Language: English
ASIN: B00OJFP1SS
Text-to-Speech: Enabled ☑
X-Ray: Not Enabled ☑
Lending: Not Enabled
Amazon Best Sellers Rank: #80,042 Paid in Kindle Store (See Top 100 Paid in Kindle Store)
    #8 in Kindle Store > Kindle eBooks > Crafts, Hobbies & Home > Animal Care & Pets > Birds
    #38 in Books > Crafts, Hobbies & Home > Pets & Animal Care > **Birds**
Would you like to **give feedback on images** or **tell us about a lower price**? .

Telling Amazon about a lower price will not automatically match prices. However, if enough people tell Amazon about the price, they will almost always lower the price. The price lowering process usually takes about a day to take effect.

I have noticed that Amazon is normally quicker to match the prices of Walmart, Target and Best Buy. This is where the Slickdeal/Fatwallet community comes in: when everyone pitches in to tell Amazon about the lower price, things move more quickly.

I find it more cost-effective to wait for Amazon to price match any deal that its main competitors are running since I save on having to pay sales tax without having to worry about dealing with resale forms. This applies to Colorado at the time of writing.

More and more states are now requiring Amazon to charge state sales tax so saving on sales tax may not apply to you, nor will this necessarily stay the same for residents of Colorado in the future.

Saving on tax aside, I also found that it is more cost-effective for me to wait for an Amazon price-match than to buy it from the deal originator. The reason is that my order is shipped free (with Prime membership) and arrives ready packed for shipping and comes right to my door.

Many times, all I have to do is to double check the contents, remove the packing slip and shipping label, then re-tape the package. Taped up, all the package needs is a new eBay shipping label and it is ready to be sent to your buyer!

The risk of holding out for Amazon to price-match is that they may not end up lowering the price and you may miss out on the original deal. If the deal is a popular deal on Slickdeals, especially if it is a Frontpage deal, and if the deal originator is one of "the Big Three", it is likely Amazon will price-match. This is when I hold out. I do not normally hold out for an Amazon price-match if it is not a Frontpage deal.

Amazon Prime Membership

In addition to offering "Free Super Saver Shipping" (FSSS), which is free shipping on almost everything with a $35 minimum purchase, Amazon also offers Prime membership (http://amazon.com/prime). At the time of writing, Amazon charges $99/year for its Prime membership.

Initially, this subscription gave you free two-day shipping with no minimum order requirements. Since the success of the Kindle however, Amazon has expanded Prime benefits to include: free viewing of many movies and TV shows with Prime Instant Video, one free book borrow per month, one free Editor's Choice book per month, and free Prime music streaming.

I was initially very hesitant to add to my costs that would cut into my profit margins, but I am now sold on this subscription. The main reason for my recommendation is that you do not need to meet the usual $35 order minimum to qualify for free shipping.

Without Prime, many deals do not meet the $35 order minimum to qualify for FSSS. After tagging on shipping charges, the "deal" quickly becomes much less of a deal and can make the difference between you making a profit or not.

With Prime membership, the problem of having shipping charges tagged onto your cost is eliminated so you only have to factor your purchase price into your inventory costs. Prime Membership costs are added into my yearly overhead charges.

Another big advantage of having Prime membership is the amazing speed at which your order arrives (usually in 2 days)! The downside is that Amazon has upped the ante so much that I think buyers have become a little too used to receiving orders so quickly that they also expect the same shipping speeds from small-time eBay sellers like myself. I digress. You will receive your Amazon Prime orders *quickly*.

The upside is that once your purchase is confirmed, you can pretty safely list your item on eBay almost immediately, with the confidence that your product will be at your doorstep in a couple of days. I have had countless instances where packages have arrived and re-shipped the same day.

Occasionally, though, the "in stock" item suddenly becomes "backordered". Usually this sudden change in stock availability is caused by Slickdealers. Sometimes, your order can be delayed by as long as 3 weeks. Depending on the item, the market for the item may change temporarily or even permanently.

Whether you want to continue with the purchase will depend on the product and your risk tolerance. Is the price of the item low? Is the potential profit margin good? Does the market demand look strong? Just like the problem of having a saturated market, waiting 3 weeks may change your profitable venture into a money-losing one.

For more details about Amazon Prime, visit: http://amzn.to/1x82uQh.

If you have a valid .edu email address, you qualify for 50% off Prime membership fees (you pay $49/year). However, you will lose some privileges like movie and video streaming. For more information, visit: http://amzn.to/1ra2Zqc.

For completeness, I will add that Amazon has another program called Amazon Mom (http://amzn.to/16Eir4T). "Mom" offered excellent resale opportunities when the program was first launched. Since then however, I have not found "Mom" to be particularly useful for me as an eBay reseller.

Amazon Kindle Special Offers

If you are reading this book, chances are, you are reading it on a Kindle. If you have a later-generation Kindle or Kindle Fire, I highly suggest signing up for "Kindle Special Offers" (KSO). You can only see and take part in KSO deals if you have a compatible Kindle.

According to Amazon's instructions, "If you have an eligible Kindle or Kindle Fire and are not already subscribed to Special Offers, you can subscribe at no charge. You can unsubscribe at any time with no additional cost.

1. Visit Manage Your Content and Devices (http://amzn.to/1Hi9RUJ).
2. Select the **Your Devices** tab.
3. Click your device to display more information.

4. Next to **Special Offers**, click **Edit**, and then click **Subscribe**.
5. The next time you connect your Kindle device wirelessly, it will complete the process of subscribing your device to Special Offers."

You can sign up for text notification of upcoming deals at http://amzn.to/1JBnG4D.

For more information about KSO, visit: http://amzn.to/1urpCpm for more information.

I do not know how long Amazon will continue offering these deals, or how good future deals would be. However, the reason I recommend signing up for KSO is because it is *free*.

From time to time, Amazon will offer very special limited deals for their KSO users. Deals are limited to one offer per Amazon account. Meaning, if you have 2 Kindles that are attached to the same Amazon account, you can only redeem *one* KSO offer.

Past deals have included an Acer laptop for $70, a Cuisinart Juicer for $20, a Kindle paperwhite for $20 and a Misfit Shine for $20. Not all deals have been good but notable ones have been worth purchasing and have been very profitable for me.

Amazon.com Rewards Visa

I do not have an Amazon credit card because it is more profitable for me to purchase Amazon gift cards from Safeway which allows me to accumulate gas points.

At Safeway's lowest 2x gas rewards on gift card offer, if I purchase $100 worth of Amazon gift cards, I get $0.20 off a gallon up to 25 gallons. That equates to $5 off a full tank of gas, which effectively gives me 5% back in the form of gas discount versus 3% points back from Amazon's credit card.

If I buy gift cards when Safeway is running a bonus gas points offer (usually 4x gas rewards) for gift card purchases, my cash back increases to 10% back in the form of gas discount + the percent cash back from the credit or debit card which I used to purchase the gift cards with.

If you do not have a grocery store chain where you can replicate my Safeway gas deal, or if you spend more at Amazon per month than you can claim back in gas rewards discounts before they expire, then using the Amazon Rewards Visa may help to pad your profits.

Amazon purchases paid with the Rewards Visa will earn you 3% points back on orders. Points can be redeemed on Amazon towards eligible purchases. They can also be redeemed for cash back, gift cards and travel. For more information, visit: http://amzn.to/1vctHuT.

Items I Look Out for on Amazon

I have to admit that it is hard to pinpoint any specific item(s) to look out for simply because Amazon carries such a vast and dizzying array of items. Over the years, I have resold everything from books to DVDs, from Rogaine (for hair regrowth) to video games, from heart rate monitors to software, from electric shavers to diapers.

My advice is to just see what Amazon deals come up on Slickdeals and compare it to the resale potential on eBay, based on eBay's Completed Listings.

IV. Staples/Office Depot/Office Max

Almost all ideas in this chapter can be applied to Office Depot/Office Max. However, I will focus on Staples because I both live close to a Staples and I have found that Staples has, for the most part, offered the most opportunities for profit. If you are a Slickdeals visitor, you will start noticing more deals from Staples rather than Office Depot/OfficeMax being posted.

Many deals posted are clearance deals that can only be found in *some* of their brick and mortar stores. Availability will depend on location in these cases. However, if you do not have a Staples store near you, many deals are also available at Staples.com. Check Slickdeals and/or Fatwallet for updated deals.

IMPORTANT:

NEVER ever mention Slickdeals or Fatwallet to anyone in store.

Please do not bring in any Slickdeals or Fatwallet printouts to "prove" to the store employees that the deal exists.

Do *NOT* bring this book in to prove your point.

Never admit to re-selling anything or admit to being a reseller.

Staples has been generous with their awesome deals. Please keep a low profile and do not ruin Staples deals for everyone else.

Couponing is not a common practice with Staples' customers and the store employees *will* remember you with your piles of coupons quickly. (By the second visit to my local store, employees, manager included, already remembered me by my full name.)

Staples Price-Matching

Staples.com will price match select online retailers like Amazon, and Staples stores. The price match will be the price after coupons and rebates. For example, if the price on Staples.com is $100 and you used a $25 coupon, and

Amazon's price is $50, Staples will only reduce the price by another $25, netting you Amazon's $50 price.

While this is not Staples' official policy, some phone representatives may allow you to apply the $25 coupon *after* the price match, which will net you the item for $25. I have found more success trying to get a coupon applied after the price-match if I talk to someone over the phone rather than through Staples.com's online chat. In fact, I have never been successful in getting the online representative to apply the coupon after price-matching.

Staples stores will price match competitor stores, their respective website prices as well as Staples.com. As with Staples.com, allowing use of coupons after price-matching will depend on the store as well as the manager on duty.

For certain promotional periods, such as their Back-to-School events, Staples has reinstituted their 110% price match guarantee. That means that they will price-match then add an additional 10% discount off the difference.

Visit http://bit.ly/1rZScgD for Staples' full price-matching policy.

Using Coupons at Staples

Couponing at Staples is an excellent way to increase profits. As far as I know, Staples accepts its own store coupons, manufacturer coupons as well as competitor coupons. I have not, however, been able to find a publicly available comprehensive official Staples coupon policy.

There are a few ways to access Staples' coupons.

- You can find new coupons every Sunday morning at http://www.staples.com/coupons. These coupons are not barcoded and can be used multiple times by multiple users. You will normally see copies of these coupons posted on Slickdeals if it is relevant to the deal posted. Coupons available online or in their weekly flyer often feature percent-off coupons. An example is their 20% off everything you can fit in their reusable tote bag. The coupon will entitle you to a free tote plus the applicable discount. Certain items like laptops, tablets, and certain brands of ink are normally excluded from the coupon offer.

- Subscribe to Staples emails. You can subscribe by making a request to Staples at http://bit.ly/1vENx2G. Emails containing special coupons are normally sent out on Monday nights. Unlike the coupons which are posted on Staples.com, the coupons you receive in your email are normally bar-coded and are only a one-time use. Different subscribers may get different offers. However, the best ones are dollar-off coupons such as $25 off a $75 or more purchase or $30 off $100 a purchase. In general, you cannot use these coupons on tablet or Kindle purchases.

- Sign up for your free Staples Rewards account at: https://www.staplesrewardscenter.com/. There is a "Coupon Wallet" within the Rewards Center with special targeted coupons.

- Some coupons released will "trigger" deals such as 25% back in Rewards. These coupons may be released via any of the above methods.

- The Staples catalog also contains coupons not usually found elsewhere. Most of the time, the coupons are dollar off coupons and only apply to breakroom supply purchases or free gift with purchase coupons. Examples are $25 off $75 in breakroom supply purchases, or free duffel or travel bag set with $100 purchase. You can sign up to have catalogs mailed to you at http://bit.ly/1q0TrXv. Catalogs are also available by the entrance or exits of Staples stores.

- Sometimes, Staples will also mail you dollar off coupons in the mail. These are often $25 off $75 coupons. I believe customers who receive these mailings are customers Staples wants to attract back to their stores. They may also mail out these coupons to the area where a new store is opening. Store opening coupons are normally $10 off any purchase coupons, valid at the new store only. The coupons I have received are normally valid for online or phone purchases only. However, my local store normally accepts them as well. A manager override is needed.

At the time of writing, the Staples in-store system will accept expired coupons up to two days after the expiration date. This is an important point because new sales prices for the week normally come out after the coupon's expiration date. Applying an expired coupon to the updated deal may net you higher profits. It is best to just write down the coupon code of expired coupons rather than handing printed coupons to the cashier who may notice the expiration date and may deny its use.

If the staff gives you strange looks with your hand-written coupons, just say you want to save on printer ink. I find that it's best to stay consistent with handwritten coupon codes. I simply always present all coupon codes, including Staples Reward Certificate codes, in handwriting. The only exceptions where I present actual coupons are coupons that I have received in the mail.

Staples may also accept competitor coupons. Their coupon policy used to be posted on Staples.com but unfortunately, it looks like they have removed it. It seems that accepting competitor coupons are at store or manager discretion. To be honest, I have never tried presenting non-direct competing store coupons like Target coupons. However, Office Depot/OfficeMax coupons have always been accepted at my local stores.

I normally get my Office Depot/OfficeMax coupons from the catalogs they mail me. You can request Office Depot/OfficeMax catalogs here: http://bit.ly/10Dy9u2.

Office Depot coupons normally consist of dollar off coupons as well, much like the $25 off $75 offers that Staples issues. However, with the merger of Office Depot and OfficeMax, it remains to be seen what the new merged company will issue.

Using In-Store Only Coupons On Online-Only Items

From time to time, Staples.com will carry online-only items which, if you could apply an in-store only coupon will net you an excellent deal. Unfortunately, Staples.com will know that the in-store coupon that you tried to apply at checkout cannot be used online.

A way to circumvent their system is to place your Staples.com order *in store*, using thier kiosk. When ordering at the kiosk, you have the option of having the order shipped to the store, or shipped to your home. At the end of the checkout process, select the "pay in store" option. The invoice will then print in-store. Bring your printout and your in-store coupon to pay. At checkout, the in-store coupon should apply since your order is now being processed in-store.

I know that this process can be a hassle and may not be worth it if you do not live near a Staples store. However, if you do live near a Staples, the effort can be worth the potential profits.

Stacking Coupons

In general, the Staples system will allow you to use a one dollar-off coupon together with one percentage-off coupon. If you have a product-specific Staples coupon, you should be able to use it as well.

Additionally, if you have a manufacturer coupon, it can be applied on top of all the other coupons. It has been a while since I have used a manufacturer coupon at Staples but you should hand the manufacturer coupon to the cashier *last*. The last time I used a manufacturer coupon, it locked up the system and made applying store coupons impossible. The whole transaction had to be canceled and re-rung up. It was not a fun process for anyone!

My store will also allow me to "stack" Staples and manufacturer coupons. Meaning the manager will allow me to use one Staples $25 off $75 as well as one $30 off $100 Office Depot coupon, as long as I make a purchase totalling $175 or more. By "stacking", I can get $55 off my $175 purchase.

Again, this may be at manager discretion. **Always be polite, easy-going and respectful to the store staff and management. A little goes a long way in helping you get your way.** Always ask nicely if they will accept competitor coupons before fishing them out.

For example, at checkout, say this to the cashier, "I read on Staples.com that you guys accept competitor coupons. It's been a while since I've checked your policy. Can you please ask your manager if I can still use my Office Depot/OfficeMax coupon on this order?"

If the answer is a "yes", and if applicable, ask if you can use the competitor coupons *with* a Staples coupon on your order. I like to add "ask the manager" in my query because it will be he/she who has the final say.

Staples deal-stacking varies from coupon to coupon, store to store, employee to employee and sometimes even time of day! If you get a "No", accept that answer. You can choose to complete the sale with the less awesome deal, or you can politely decline the purchase. If you feel obligated to complete the purchase regardless, you can return most items within 14 days. I find it the least hassle to politely decline the purchase if the final deal becomes unprofitable without a coupon "stack". Know your price limits before you enter the store.

That said, I have never personally encountered a store manager at Staples who has not been obliging. My experience applies to stores in the Greater-Denver, Colorado area as well as to stores in Albuquerque, New Mexico. My assumption based on my experience, is that it is corporate policy to keep the customer happy - and it works! In my view, Staples beats Office Depot/OfficeMax, hands down.

Rebates

Rebates and coupons are the bread and butter of Staples. Staples is also the only company that I know of that offers "easy rebates".

Basically, instead of having to cut out and mail UPCs and rebate forms to a rebate processing center, Staples allows you to do everything online. No cutting, postage stamps or mailing needed. SERs can be submitted online at: http://bit.ly/1wQgRGU. If you ordered an item in store at the kiosk, select "Ordered at a computer terminal in store" when you are submitting your SER.

The only rebate that I have come across where you cannot use the Staples Easy Rebate (SER) process has been for McAfee Software rebates. McAfee rebates have to be redeemed the traditional way - by mail.

Staples often runs free-after-rebate (FAR) deals. Common FAR offer items include antivirus software, paper reams and/or cases of paper, stationery (these offers are usually held during their Back To School promotions). Many of these are also SER offers which saves on effort and mailing costs.

You can normally submit your in-store purchase rebates immediately. You may need to wait up to 24 hours for the rebate system to recognize online or kiosk purchase order numbers. SERs can be tracked online and often take 4-6 weeks to be processed.

Rebates can come in the form of payment to your Paypal account (usually for stationary rebates totalling less than $10), by pre-paid Visa cards, Staples gift cards, or by rebate check. Often, Staples will provide you with the default option of a prepaid card rebate but which you have the option of requesting a check instead.

If there is a Paypal payout option, the default payment option offered is usually in the form of a check. You will not incur a Paypal charge if you choose Paypal as your rebate redemption option.

Making A Profit After Rebate

Using gift cards, coupons or Rewards at Staples does not reduce the promised rebate amount. It is possible and easy to make money off a FAR deal. Here is an example of how it works: let's say Staples runs a FAR deal on a $90 Norton anti-virus software. In theory, you are expected to pay the full $90 out of your pocket then submit the rebate to claim your $90 back.

However, you can use your dollars-off coupon in the deal. If you have a $25 off $75 coupon, you would instead only have paid $65 but you will still get $90 back in the form of a rebate. Net profit = $25. If you have a $30 off $100 coupon, you will need to purchase an additional $10 worth of merchandise to reach the $100 minimum.

Let's say you found something you needed, maybe two packs of packing tape, and you spent $105 total instead. Less the $30 off $100 coupon, your out of pocket expenditure is $75. Your rebate check is still $90. Net profit = $15 + $15 worth of packing tape. You can also apply the percent-off coupon with the same effect. If you have both, you will increase your profits accordingly.

Since using a gift card or Staples Rewards will not reduce the rebate amount, taking advantage of FAR deals is a good way of getting cash out of your gift cards or Rewards certificates.

Staples Rewards

Maximize your profits by signing up for a free Staples Rewards membership at http://bit.ly/1x82Q9t. In addition to receiving free shipping with no minimum order requirements, you will also earn up to 5% back in Rewards on all purchases in-store or online. You will earn Rewards regardless of payment method. However, you do not earn Rewards on purchases paid with Reward certificates.

Basic membership will earn you 2% back in Rewards on most purchases. If you spend $500 in a calendar year, you will be upgraded to Plus membership which earns you 3% back in rewards on most purchases, while Premier members will get 5% back on most purchases.

You will need to spend at least $1000 in a calendar year to reach the Premier level. Upgraded memberships are valid for one year. Then, your membership reverts to the Basic membership until you meet the spending threshold again. Purchases made with Rewards do not count towards the spending minimums.

Believe it or not, it is very easy to reach the $1000 needed to Premier. Taking advantage of all their FAR deals will help you reach that amount quickly with little to no money spent. If you followed my methods, you should have already made a profit while working your way to that $1000 mark.

You can also be automatically bumped up to the Plus/Premier level if you are approved for the Staples Business Account. I do not think having a Staples Business

Account is necessary. For more information, visit: http://bit.ly/1urpSVj.

Rewards are issued on a monthly basis if a Basic member earns at least $10 or if Plus/Premier members earn at least $5. Otherwise, Rewards are rolled into the subsequent month until the applicable minimum is reached. Rewards can be used online or in the store.

For online redemptions, any amounts unclaimed will remain in your account until it is fully used or expires. For in-store redemptions, any unused amounts will be reissued in the form of a barcoded receipt, which is printed under your purchase receipt.

For example, if you have $12 in Rewards and you only spent $10, the checkstand will print you a $2 Reward receipt which you can use next time. However, if you then spend $1.50 the next time and use that $2 Reward receipt, you will lose the remaining $0.50. A new receipt will not be printed for the remaining amount.

If you return the item that you purchased using your Rewards, Staples should reissue the Rewards amount by printing you a new Rewards receipt. In theory, you should get a new Rewards printout as long as the Rewards have not expired at the time of the return.

This, however does not always happen and may require some finessing on the part of the manager. Always remember to be patient and polite. If the Rewards have expired, you will not get a new printout and you will lose the Rewards.

Free After Rewards

Free After Rewards is similar to Free After Rebates except instead of getting a monetary rebate refund or a Staples gift card, you will get back the amount you paid in the form of Rewards. Unlike rebate offers, Free After Rewards are often applied instantly with limits, as in the Reward amount is automatically added to your account after purchase.

Depending on the offer, you may be allowed to receive a limit of one or two Rewards that will be applied to your account. Additional purchases will not net you the Reward amount. Rewards normally expire more quickly than other rebate forms so be sure you use them in time!

Free After Rewards items normally include batteries and stationery items like folders. Additionally, you cannot "roll" Rewards. That means that if you paid for your deal with Staples Rewards, you will not receive any further Rewards back into your account.

If you paid with coupons, the coupon amount will be deducted from the Reward amount. You will not get the full price in Rewards back. For example, if the batteries are $12 for a pack, you should get $12 back in Rewards.

However, if you used a $5 Reward coupon and only paid $7 for the batteries, you will only receive $7 back in Rewards. Similarly, if you bought $12 worth of batteries and used a 20% off coupon, your out-of-pocket cost is $9.60. Your Reward amount will be $9.60 and not $12.

Never waste your coupons or Rewards! Use only gift cards or cash/check/credit card payments for Free After Rewards deals. If applicable, you can still maximize your returns by using Staples gift cards purchased from grocery stores for gas rewards. Cash in your gift card balance(s) and/or Staples rewards with FAR deals.

The Ink Recycling Program

The ink recycling program is an excellent way for you to earn Staples Rewards. In order to participate in the program, you will need to have made at least $30 in ink purchases within the previous 180 days.

Inks can be purchased at once, or in separate purchases. Staples will only consider the amount you paid out of pocket. That is, if you used a coupon or Rewards, the amount that you saved will not be applied to your $30 minimum.

If you are making ink purchases solely to meet the $30 minimum, do not use any Rewards or coupons when you check out. If you have coupons and/or Rewards to use and are purchasing more than ink, purchase your ink in a separate transaction so that you can hit your ink purchase requirement without getting confused by any additional coupon/reward discounts.

You can purchase ink and recycle on the same day in-store. If you are ordering ink online, you should wait until the ink order is shipped before recycling your inks so that your account will be credited properly.

Once you have made the required ink purchase, you can recycle your used ink cartridges in return for Staples Rewards. Staples will give you $2 in rewards for every cartridge you recycle, up to 10 cartridges per month ($20 in rewards) if you are a Basic member or up to 20 cartridges per month ($40 in rewards) if you are a Plus/Premier member. Staples will accept any type of ink or toner cartridge for recycling.

You can recycle your empty cartridges in-store or online. If you do not have a store close by, submit your ink cartridges to Staples by mail. Log into your Staples account at http://tinyurl.com/ntnx2sh. Choose the "Recycle Ink and Toner" option and you can then create a free shipping label for your cartridges.

If you are lucky, your workplace or friend's/relative's workplace can be a goldmine of cartridges that nobody knows what to do with. Offer to recycle the inks for them and be a hero! You can also post a Want Ad on Craigslist for used ink. You can say you need it for a project.

You may be more successful with such an ad if you live in, or close to a metropolitan area. For completeness, I will add you can also try your luck "fishing" for used ink cartridges at ink recycle bins. However, I am not responsible or liable if you get into trouble for your "fishing expeditions"!

If all else fails, you can purchase empty ink cartridges in bulk on eBay. The average price is about $0.12/used cartridge if you buy a big lot. Buying used inks is not the most profitable option but a viable one. If applicable, be sure to accumulate gas points by buying eBay gift cards from one of the sources I listed in the Gift Card chapter for your ink purchase.

Back To School (BTS)

Staples' BTS season usually runs between mid-June and mid-September, with most deals running in August. During this time, Staples will heavily promote their BTS pass for $10. They will ask you if you want to purchase a pass every time you checkout.

The BTS pass entitles you to 15% off BTS supplies such as notebooks, paper and backpacks during the BTS period. Some cashiers may even try the hard-sell approach, telling you that the BTS pass will basically pay for itself when you spend more than $67 in BTS items.

Using the BTS pass will affect your rebates and use of other coupons. Do not purchase it unless you fully understand Staples' deals and coupon stacking. I have never purchased a pass. I think it is a waste of $10 and do not recommend it. Stick to the Ink Rewards.

An Example of Reselling A Deal from Staples

Here is a real-world example of reselling an item that you "extreme-couponed" at Staples. The Keurig K10 Mini Plus K-cup Brewer regularly retails for $99.

The item is on sale at Staples for $75 with a $10 manufacturer rebate and a $15 Staples Easy Rebate which you get back in the form of a Staples gift card. Use the $25 off $75 breakroom supply coupon from the catalogs that are at the entrance/exit of the store.

In the past, I have been able to stack a 20% off coupon as well, but we will not consider the 20% in this example. Use your Staples Rewards to pay the balance, or use the Staples gift card which you purchased using your cash-back credit/debit card at the grocery store.

If you used your Staples Rewards to pay the balance, your out-of-pocket costs = $0, or the price of your used inks, if you purchased them. Staples in my area does not add sales tax when I use my rewards to completely pay for the item. I am not sure if it applies to all states.

What you got after rebate:
Keurig K10 brewer +
$15 Staples gift card +
$10 manufacturer rebate check.

The out-of-pocket costs if you used a gift card purchased from the grocery store = $50 in gift card value.

What you got after rebate:
Keurig K10 brewer +
$15 Staples gift card +
$10 manufacturer rebate check +
At least $0.10 off/gallon of gas (more if you purchased the gift card during a bonus gas points period) +
$0.50 credit/debit card cash back (which you used to buy the gift card with. You might get air miles or a higher cash-back rate, depending on your card) +
2-5% back in Rewards (depending on your Reward tier)

The out-of-pocket costs if you used a gift card purchased from a discounted gift card website like cardpool = $47.50 in cash outlay to buy a $50 gift card at 5% discount.

What you got after rebate:
Keurig K10 brewer +
$15 Staples gift card +
$10 manufacturer rebate check +
$0.48 credit/debit card cash back (which you used to buy the gift card with. You might get air miles or a higher cash-back rate, depending on your card) +
2-5% back in Rewards (depending on your Reward tier)

Selling the Keurig K10 on eBay = $89.95 with free shipping
Shipping cost = $15 (approximately)
eBay fees = $9
Paypal fees = $3.34
Cost of Keurig K10 = $50 (at the highest out-of-pocket-price)
Net profit = *at least* $12.61 + $10 check rebate + $15 Staples gift card SER + any other cashback and/or gas savings + 2-5% back in Rewards.

If you were able to apply a 20% off coupon, your profit increases by $10. If you paid with Ink Rewards, your profit jumps to the full $62.61 plus almost all the extras. If you paid for the Keurig fully with Rewards, you will not earn the 2-5% back in Rewards.

This example can be applied to many items at Staples. By stacking deals in various forms, I have gotten everything from a $500 laptop for $100, multitudes of printers for $20 or less (usually free because they were paid with Rewards), made money on more cases of multi-purpose and photo paper than I can possibly ever use, multiple coffee brewers at a fifth of their retail price and cartons full of free batteries.

Keeping Up to Date on Staples' Deals

Check Slickdeals Staples thread (http://bit.ly/1oKkxCP) and go to the last page for the latest offers.

Items I Look Out for at Staples

Good resale items to look out for at Staples include clearance cameras, laptops, tablets, money-making or free-after-rebate software, Keurig coffee brewers and pods and printers. Other items that I look out for at Staples are items that I can use for eBay business including paper and packing tape.

V. Kohl's/Macy's/Dillard's

Again, some ideas in this chapter may be applied to the other department stores. However, I will focus on Kohl's. I started deal-hunting at Kohl's much later in my eBay selling "career".

At the time of writing, Kohl's has been an eBay source for me for about 5 years. However, Kohl's/kohls.com has rapidly become one of *the* go-to stores for my eBay inventory. I make most of my purchases online rather than in-store.

At first glance, Kohl's pricing is high - *very* high. Their MSRP prices are normally marked up by at least a third more than discount retailers like Target. I once found an infant jumpsuit retailing at Kohl's for $24. That exact jumpsuit was sold at Sam's Club for under $8. That said, you can score awesome deals, if you know how to play the Kohl's game.

Variable Pricing

Kohl's/kohls.com pricing is almost never static. Items will often go on sale before jumping back to their original inflated price. The price may then stay at the original price but with a buy-one-get-one-free deal, or a buy-one-get-one-half-off deal. Their sale prices will coincide with their 15%-20%-30% off deals and Kohl's Cash (KC) offers.

The best deals are sale/clearanced-priced items stacked with a coupon deal. Sales with percent-discount codes and KC are usually conducted bi-weekly and run for 6 days.

Price-Matching At Kohl's

Both Kohl's and kohls.com will price-match. Kohl's official policy is that they will price-match instore only but not at kohls.com. However, I have never had a phone representative tell me that I could not price match an item.

If you are price-matching an item in-store, you will need to bring the current competitor ad, with the price you want to match. I have also been able to price-match using computer printouts of online sales run by reputable retailers.

If you have a printout, be prepared to spend some time waiting for the manager to verify the sale price. Since there is no publicly available official policy on using printouts for price-matching, nor was I able to find out which retailers they will price-match to, I cannot say with certainty that what has worked for me will work for you.

If you are pre-matching an item online, you will need the SKU number of your kohls.com item (you will need to add the item to your Shopping Bag in order to see the SKU number), as well as the competitor's website and item number.

The phone representative will then verify the price and item before applying the price-match. The process is slow so be sure you have the time to be on hold, and be sure to have the kohls.com SKU ready to help speed things up.

In the past, I have price-matched items from many retailers including Tuesday Morning, Costco, Amazon, Best Buy and Walmart.

You can request a price-adjustment if you find a lower price for an item within 14 days of purchase. You will need your receipt if you are price-adjusting in-store, or your order number if you are price adjusting an online order. If the item is on clearance, you will probably need to return and repurchase the item at the clearance price.

Coupons

The heart of reselling Kohl's/kohls.com items lies in couponing. Kohl's often releases 10%, 20% or 30% off coupons that can be applied to almost all items, including sale and clearance-priced items. Items like some video game consoles are not eligible for coupon discounts. Coupons are printed on catalogs which are sent to customers. The percent-off amounts are targeted.

You may receive a 15%, 20% or 30% coupon in your catalog. Unless you are a big Kohl's spender, or unless Kohl's wants you back as a customer, you will normally receive a 15% or 20% off coupon. It is easier to get the 30% off coupon code for kohls.com from Slickdeals than to get the 30% off coupon in the mail. In most cases, you can only use the 30% off coupon if you have a Kohl's Charge Card.

Stacking Coupons

During each promotion period, Kohl's often has more than one promotional code which will earn you a percentage of discount back. If you have two discount codes: GIFTING20 which gives you 20% off your order, and code GIFTING25, which gives you 25% off a purchase of $100 or more, only the best code will apply.

That is, if you have an order of $99, code GIFTING20 will apply. If your order is $105, code GIFTING25 will apply. Kohls.com will not apply both codes to your order.

However, kohls.com also has department-specific discount codes. They may, for example, have codes for 30% off Britax car seats or 20% off menswear. These codes can be stacked with total order percent-discount codes. Similarly, dollar-off department-specific codes like $10 off $30 kids items can be stacked with total order percent-discount codes.

Kohls.com normally offers free shipping with a minimum purchase of $50 or $75 (depending on the offer). Additionally, they also often offer free shipping codes (no minimum purchase required). Some free shipping codes can only be applied by Kohl's Charge card holders. While you can stack some coupons, kohls.com used to only allow you to enter two coupons plus a free shipping coupon code.

Manufacturer and Competitor Coupons

Kohls.com will not accept manufacturer or competitor coupons. However, the brick and mortar stores will accept them at store discretion. I have never used manufacturer coupons at Kohls.

However, Kohl's has accepted both Costco booklet coupons as well as Bed Bath and Beyond 20% off coupons. You can get these 20% off coupons in most Home and Garden magazines. Bed Bath and Beyond will also often send you these coupons in the mail. It seems that my local Kohls stores allow cashiers to accept the Bed Bath and Beyond coupons without manager approval.

The Costco coupons, however, required manager approval. Your success rate may vary, depending on the store.

Stacking Coupons *and* Price-Matching Deals

Kohl's will allow you to stack price-matching deals with coupons. After a price-match, you should also be allowed to apply your Kohl's coupon to an order. As far as I know, the official policy is that you if you have a coupon, you can only get an additional 15% off after price-match.

I have, however, had success applying 30% off coupons after price match. If you are attempting to stack a deal online, you will need to call kohls.com to process the price match. Follow the process that I outlined in the kohls.com price-matching section.

After you have successfully price-matched, give your phone representative your coupon codes. I will provide them will all the coupon codes that I have. This can include percent-off purchase codes, department specific discount codes and/or free shipping codes.

Always give them the code with the highest percent-off first, which is usually 30% off. The representative may deny your request and tell you that the maximum discount you can apply is a 15% off coupon after price-match. They may automatically apply that discount for you, but I suggest that you also have a 15% off code ready.

Depending on the deal or how much time you have, you can either complete the sale, or your may wish to cancel the order and try another representative. This process is time-consuming, especially if you are attempting to connect to a more obliging phone representative.

If it is a limited-supply or clearance deal that hit the Frontpage on Slickdeals, you may run the risk of the item selling out before the order is finalized.

I have found that stacking a price-match + a 30% coupon is easier in store. After the store manager has approved the price-match, try to wait for them to leave. Then present your 30% off coupon to the cashier. You will need the physical coupon from the catalog. Some cashiers may accept a copy or printout.

If you don't have a physical coupon, try asking the Slickdeals forum for a scanned copy before leaving for the store. I have never had any issue getting the maximum discount off after price-match in-store. Again, your experience may be different depending on the store. I do not know if Kohl's will allow you to use a competitor coupon after a price matching. I suppose it wouldn't hurt to try. The most they can do is say no.

Kohl's Cash (KC)

When Kohl's runs its 15%, 20%, or 30% off promotion, you will also have the chance to earn Kohl's Cash. Let's say the Kohl's Cash earning period is between 9/10 and 9/17. The redemption period will then be between 9/18 and 9/28. Earning opportunity dates as well as redemption dates will be advertised at both kohls.com as well as in their print mailers. The redemption period may coincide with the next earning period.

According to Kohl's, "Kohl's Cash is not legal tender or transferable. You will receive a $10 Kohl's Cash coupon for the first $50 purchased. An additional $10 in value will be added to the coupon for each additional $50 spent in that single transaction.

Multiple transactions cannot be combined to qualify or increase the amount of Kohl's Cash earned. Kohl's Cash is earned on the amount purchased after all applicable discounts are applied and before tax is imposed. Eligible customer purchases include sale-, regular- and clearance-priced merchandise purchased during the event's earn dates, but exclude the purchase of gift cards."

Kohl's Cash can be earned and redeemed in stores or online. Kohl's Cash certificates have short redemption dates. You have to redeem your Kohl's Cash within the specified timeframe for online orders.

However, many if not most stores will accept expired Kohl's Cash at store discretion. Kohl's Cash may not be redeemed to purchase Kohl's Cares for Kids® merchandise or other charitable items, to reduce a Kohl's Charge or any third party charge account balance, as price adjustments on prior purchases or to purchase gift cards.

You will not earn Kohl's Cash on the portion of the order that was paid with Kohl's Cash. For example, if your order was $50 and you used $10 Kohl's Cash to pay for part of the order, the amount you paid out of pocket amount is $40. You will not be able to earn any additional Kohl's Cash until you spend an additional $10 (ie $60 including the Kohl's Cash payment).

Percent-off discounts will not stack with Kohl's Cash. Meaning, if you have a 30% off coupon applied to a $100 order, you will get $30 off your order and your final price will be $70. However, if you redeemed $20 in Kohl's Cash from a previous deal, you will only get 30% off $80 or $24 off your order. You do not get the full $30 off because of the Kohl's Cash redemption.

If you want to circumvent the problems associated with using Kohl's Cash, this is what I recommend: purchase something to use up the full value of your Kohl's Cash. Return this item immediately. When you return the item, Kohl's will refund your Kohl's Cash in the form of merchandise credit. Your $10 (or whatever amount) worth of Kohl's Cash is now the equivalent amount in Kohl's merchandise credit.

Kohl's merchandise credit functions like a gift card and does not expire. Additionally, when you pay using merchandise credit, the *full* discount will be taken off your total. Thus, in my previous example, if you now made your purchase partially with your merchandise credit, you will get the full $30 off a $100 order with the 30% off coupon.

If you return part or all of an order that earned you the Kohl's Cash which you have already redeemed, Kohl's will deduct the Kohl's Cash you redeemed from your refund amount. If you did not redeem your Kohl's Cash then they will refund you the full amount paid.

Kohl's Charge Card

The Kohl's Charge Card is the only department store charge card that I have. I decided to apply for a Charge Card after losing out on the best (30% off) deals and do not regret it. Many 30% off discount codes will only apply if you have a Kohl's Charge Card. Kohl's Charge Card holders also often get free shipping or free shipping codes.

You do not need to use your Charge Card to to be able to use any of the Charge holder codes. As long as you have a Charge Card associated with your online account, you can use the 30% off code(s) even if you pay with a gift card or merchandise credit.

Kohl's brick and mortar stores may require you to use your Charge Card in order to use your 30% off code. You can sidestep this problem, and maximize profits by asking the cashier to charge $1 on your Kohl's Charge then use your gift card/merchandise credit to pay for the rest of the order.

In both cases, either online or in-store, apply my gift card and/or merchandise credit stacking tricks to maximize your profits.

Kohl's Emails

Sign up for Kohl's emails at http://tinyurl.com/lszxon2. You will receive a 15% off coupon after you sign up. However, I suggest waiting for a better coupon. 15% off is the lowest percent-off coupon that Kohl's generates.

If you sign up for sales alerts, Kohl's will on occasion, send you one-time use discount codes which can include high-discount offers like $25 off a $50 or more purchase, or coupons for 40% off your total purchase (one-time use).

Yes2You Rewards

Kohl's has recently launched a new rewards program, Yes2You Rewards. You can earn 1 point for every dollar spent on eligible items, with special bonus point earning opportunities. For every 100 points you earn, you will receive $5 in Kohl's Cash, ie 5% back in Kohl's Cash. If you return an item, you will lose any points earned on the return.

According to Kohl's, to get your points:

In Store - If you are paying with your Kohl's Charge Card in store or online, you'll automatically be recognized as a *Yes2You* Rewards member. If you're making an in-store purchase with another form of payment, the Associate can look up your *Yes2You* Rewards number using the email address or phone number you enrolled with.

Online - After completing your *Yes2You* Rewards profile, make sure you are signed in to your Kohls.com Shopping Account when you place an order, and you'll automatically be recognized as a *Yes2You* Rewards member. Since we do not charge your order until it ships, points will be awarded within 24-48 hours after your order ships.

If you forgot your *Yes2You* Rewards card when you made your last purchase, you'll automatically be awarded points if you used your Kohl's Charge. If you didn't pay with your Kohl's Charge, please contact Customer Service at (855) 564-5705.

You will not earn points on amounts paid for with Kohl's Cash. Points expire one year after they were issued. Points can be donated or shared with other Yes2You Rewards members. You will be able to earn points if you use my trick covered in the Kohl's Cash section to extract merchandise credit from your Kohl's Cash.

Join Yes2You for free here: http://bit.ly/WHqvgx.

Rebates

Kohl's offers items for sale with manufacturer's mail-in rebates. Rebate deals are usually offered during the pre-Christmas season. Rebate offers do not affect deal and/or coupon stacking. In the past, manufacturers including Kitchenaid, Dyson, Cuisinart and Keurig have offered rebate offers that can help boost your profit margins.

Keeping Up to Date on Kohl's Deals

Keep up to date on the latest Kohl's deals on Slickdeals here: http://bit.ly/1uPmBQZ. Kohl's threads on Slickdeals are often retired to keep the thread from getting too long. Go to the last page of the thread for the latest updates, or for the link to the new thread.

Items I Look Out for at Kohl's

Items that I look out for at Kohl's include brand-name clothing, brand-name kid's clothing, toys, video games and items that are rarely discounted elsewhere like Kitchenaid kitchen appliances and Dyson products.

VI. Target

I have to admit that I love Target. A cooler, trendier version of Walmart, Target offers a big range of attractively designed, store-exclusive products.

Price-Matching at Target

Target will price match identical items from the following competitors: Target.com, Amazon.com, Walmart.com, BestBuy.com, ToysRUs.com, BabiesRUs.com or in a competitor's local printed ad. You can price match at the time of purchase or within 7 days after the purchase.

The competitor price must be current at the time of the match. If you are price-matching after purchase, you will need to present the original receipt to get your purchase matched. Visit http://bit.ly/KjAVvW for Target's full price-matching policy.

Target.com does not price-match. They will only price-adjust items if you find a lower price in the Target weekly ad or Target.com within the same week, or the week following your purchase.

Stacking Deals at Target

In addition to price-matching, Target will accept Target and manufacturer coupons. They will also accept manufacturer coupons even if it is branded with another store's logo (for example, if you received a manufacturer coupon from Safeway's Catalina, that coupon may sometimes bear Safeway's logo).

You can use one Target coupon and one manufacturer coupon per *purchase*. A purchase equates to an item and not a transaction. One transaction can consist of many purchases. That means for example, if you have two $5 off a Star Wars DVD, you can use both $5 off coupons if you buy two Star Wars DVDs in one transaction.

You can refer to Target's full coupon policy at http://bit.ly/1xQKarg. Unfortunately, Target's employees do not always know corporate policy very well. I recommend having printouts of both policies on hand when you embark on your deal-stacking attempts.

You can print Target coupons at http://bit.ly/1w650le. Target mobile coupons are available at http://cartwheel.target.com/. Manufacturer coupons can be found at http://www.coupons.com/, http://smartsource.com, http://redplum.com, http://hopster.com and http://savingstar.com.com.

Disney DVD coupons can be found at http://disneymovierewards.go.com. Each site will allow you to print up to two of the same coupon per computer. Additionally, you can find manufacturer coupons in your Sunday paper inserts.

If you use a Target coupon, a manufacturer coupon and do a price-match, the Target coupon will be applied *before* the price-match while the manufacturer coupon will be applied *after* the price-match.

Target REDcard

If you make Target one of your sources, I recommend signing up for a REDcard. You can apply for a REDcard Credit Card or a REDcard Debit Card that is linked to your existing checking account.

Getting the REDcard Debit Card means that your credit need not get pulled in order to take advantage of REDcard perks which include an additional 5% off all purchases at Target and Target.com, free shipping at Target.com and an extra 30-day window for returns. Target has a 90-day standard return policy.

You can sign up for a REDcard at http://bit.ly/1oyDn0r.

Items I Look Out for at Target

Good items to look out for for resale include: clearance items, fourth quarter (pre-Christmas season) sale items and Target-exclusive DVDs and video games with Target-exclusives.

VII. Walmart

I am not a fan of Walmart. I rarely find good resale deals here. However, for the sake of completeness, I will include a small chapter on Walmart.

Price-Matching at Walmart

Walmart will price-match any local competitor's ad pricing. They will not match online pricing. Walmart claims that you do not need to have a print ad for them to honor a price-match. My experience price-matching anything other than groceries at Walmart, however, has always been a long, drawn out, time-consuming and painful affair.

A good deal is one that does not require vast amounts of time and effort to get. Dealing with Walmart means that I need to have a bigger profit margin to compensate me for my time and hassle. I do not bother with trying to get deals by price-matching at Walmart. Walmart's full price-matching policy can be found at http://bit.ly/1e48lwt.

Walmart accepts manufacturer, competitor and Catalina coupons. You should be able to use manufacturer or Catalina coupons *after* a price-match. You can find Walmart's full coupon policy at http://bit.ly/1oaYucf.

Walmart Savings Catcher

Walmart has recently introduced its new Savings Catcher program. It is basically an automatic price-matching program where you signup and enter your receipt number at https://savingscatcher.walmart.com/. The program is only for in-store purchases.

Walmart will then compare the prices of eligible items to weekly print and digital ads of top retailers in your area. If the app "catches" a lower price, they will automatically issue you a refund of the difference in the form of a digital gift card.

Additionally, they will also give you double the difference back if you redeem the savings through your American Express Bluebird account. You can sign up at http://bit.ly/1u6DEJ6. The double the difference back offer is valid until 2/28/15. Using manufacturer coupons will not decrease the amount of the price-match.

If you make Walmart one of your inventory sources, it will be worthwhile to sign up for the program since you can potentially increase your profits with relatively little extra effort.

Items I Look Out for at Walmart

I normally look out for Walmart-exclusive releases of DVDs and video games with Walmart exclusives. I also keep an eye out for seasonal clearance items and fourth quarter sale items at Walmart.com.

VIII. Other Retailers

In addition to the retailers listed above, here are a list of retailers, together with good resale items to keep an eye out for, on Slickdeals:

- 6pm.com: Brand name shoes.

- BN.com (Barnes & Noble): Fourth quarter sales on games, books and movies. During this period, Barnes & Noble may issue coupons as high as 40% off your order. Some coupons may be category-specific (for example, for use on toy and game purchases only).

- Cowboom.com (part of Best Buy): Refurbished electronics.

- Dell.com: TVs and laptops. Many deals include a Dell e-gift card offer. For example, buy a 50" LED Smart TV for $550, get a $200 Dell e-gift card. These e-gift cards have a fairly short expiration date and can only be used on dell.com. However, there are good deals to be had. The e-gift cards can be bought and sold on eBay at below face value.

- Frys.com/Frys: Free-after-rebate software and computer components (there is no need to know what they are in order to sell them. Just check to see if the item sells in the Completed Listing search).

- Microsoft.com: Xbox game sales. These are usually held in the fourth quarter.

- Newegg.com: Free-after-rebate software and computer components.

- REI.com: Closeout/end-of-season outdoor gear and equipment.

- Toysrus.com/Toys R Us: Toys R Us exclusives. Fourth quarter sales on toys and video games. The best deals are usually Buy-One-Get-One-Free deals.

Brick and Mortar Stores:

- Gamestop: Gamestop exclusives, including pre-order exclusives. Clearance on popular video game titles like Halo, Assassin's Creed, Bioshock etc. Basically any title that they made sequels to are good bets. Keep up-to-date on video game deals at http://cheapassgamer.com.

- Goodwill and other thrift stores: Out-of-Print/Production books and toys. Look in particular for Legos and themed toys like Star Wars, comic book heroes like Batman and Spider-Man, Lord of the Rings etc. I also know of eBayers that make a good living reselling Goodwill's clothes by the pound.

- Home Depot/Lowe's: Seasonal clearance items. I do not resell items from home improvement stores often because of the big and heavy nature of their stock. The home improvement stores can, however, be a possible source for you to consider.

- TJ Maxx/Tuesday Morning/Ross: Factory seconds on popular brands. You might also find out-of-print/production toys and books here.

13 THINKING OUTSIDE THE BOX

The sum of the parts of an item is sometimes worth more than its whole. In order to maximize your profits, you will also need to "think outside the box".

For example, I used to sell a lot of video games. My favorite items to resell were collectible editions that were on sale or being clearanced out. These editions usually include the game plus other collectibles like figurines, special collector edition-only download codes, as well as other items like medals or coins that may be relevant to the game.

Here is an example of a deal that came up at the time of writing - Dark Souls II Collector's Edition on sale at Amazon for $30. A new sealed set sells on eBay for about $65.

The set includes:
- Retail copy of Dark Souls II (Xbox 360)
- Premium quality 12" tall Warrior Knight figurine, packed inside a display box
- Exclusive hardbound art book
- Full-color microfiber game map
- Black Armor edition metal base
- Original game soundtrack

If you split the set up and sold it separately, the figurine alone sells for about $40, the art book sells for about $16 (on average), the game map sells for about $10, video game (disc-only) sells for about $22, the metal case + soundtrack sells for about $10. Total selling price ~ $98 vs $65. Of course if you break up the set, you also increase the risk of one or some of the items not selling. However, you have also increased your profit potential by 33%.

In another example, I purchased a printer from Staples at a clearance price of about $65. Selling the printer itself, brand new, would not have given me a profit after all fees and commissions were factored in.

However, at that time, Staples was giving a $50 trade-in credit on used printers. Instead of selling the printer on eBay, I traded the printer in and sold the ink cartridges on eBay for about $50.

Thinking outside the box can be applied to many things from breaking sets up to sell separately, to taking a vehicle apart and selling the parts for a greater profit.

14 THE FOURTH QUARTER

The fourth quarter, known as Q4 in financial circles, consists of the final three months of the year. This is includes Black Friday (the big sales day after Thanksgiving), as well as Christmas. It is the best time for the retail sector and as long as you are ready for it, it should be the best time for you as an eBay reseller as well.

If you ship internationally, you will start to see an upswing in foreign sales starting in late October tapering off around mid-November. Sales within the US usually start increasing in November and may increase until about 7 days before Christmas.

If you offer Express Guaranteed shipping, you may get some last minute shoppers to as late as 2 days before Christmas. Christmas Eve and Christmas Day will be very slow. Depending on the economy, you may see an increase in sales a few days after Christmas - this is when people may be redeeming eBay gift cards they received, or they may be looking for the item they wanted, but did not get for Christmas.

Be Prepared

To be successful during the fourth quarter, it is extremely important that you are prepared. This includes being liquid, having plenty of mailing supplies on hand and setting aside more time to monitor Slickdeals, buy items, list on eBay, and to pack and ship.

If you are serious about finding Black Friday deals for the Christmas rush, you will need to check Slickdeals **ALL.THE.TIME.** It would be a good idea to start your Slickdeal vigil at around 5 pm EST on Thanksgiving Day.

Yes, I know that will interrupt your Thanksgiving dinner but maximizing sales and profits is not always easy. My vigils have extended from Thanksgiving through to Cyber Monday with naps in between.

Customers will also get very anxious this time of year so make sure that you stay on top of your orders and shipments during this time. Keep customers happy by aiming to ship within one business day.

Why I Do Not Camp Outside Retailers On Thanksgiving

Do you know that I have never camped outside a retailer to get a hold of Black Friday "doorbusters"? Camping out for Black Friday Doorbuster deals is for amateurs. Professional eBay resellers do not need to camp out to get those deals.

Why do I say that? This is never publicised but I will tell you that almost all the retailers I have dealt with will offer similar, if not *better* deals before Black Friday. These deals may be found online and/or in store.

In the last 5-6 years, my retail sources: Best Buy, Walmart, Target and Kohl's have all offered "doorbuster" sales at equal or *lower* prices within the 10 days *preceding* Black

Friday. Sometimes, stores like Best Buy will offer "doorbuster" deals a little earlier,they will then suspend the offer in anticipation of Black Friday. Amazon may also aggressively price-match all these retailers during this period. Keep a close watch for deals in store flyers and on Slickdeals.

Camping out on Black Friday is absolutely unnecessary when you can get that same deal as early as 2 weeks before Black Friday, shipped to your door, with the push of a few computer buttons.

My Main Black Friday Source - Amazon

What if you want to use my profit-maximizing tricks using gift cards but you are still getting your feet wet? If you want to buy retailer gift cards in advance of your fourth quarter purchasing, I recommend going with Amazon gift cards.

I recommend betting on making Amazon purchases in the fourth quarter because not only does Amazon run its own Black Friday Countdown deals, Black Friday deals and Cyber Monday deals, it also aggressively matches the Black Friday deals of its major brick and mortar competitors including: Walmart, Target, Best Buy and Sears. If there is something on sale at one of these stores, you can bet that Amazon will likely match their price quickly if they have not already done so.

Keep in mind that Amazon's pricing may fluctuate depending on their competitor's online stock. That is to say if for example, bestbuy.com shows that its $50 iPad deal is "out of stock online", Amazon may raise its price since it no longer needs to match Best Buy's offer. If you want to maximize profits, you will need to be prepared with your gift cards ready on hand to buy deals as they appear. Add the gift card credits to your Amazon account in advance which will make the ordering process go more quickly.

Deals often sell out very quickly during this time, especially after it has been on Slickdeals. Have enough gift cards on hand that you feel comfortable holding. If you are a novice, or if you have a low risk tolerance, I suggest that you have no more than $100 tied up in gift cards. Always do what feels comfortable to you and your situation.

The fourth quarter is when Amazon Prime proves its value to me as an eBay reseller. With no purchase minimums to qualify for free shipping, you do not have to worry about shipping charges ruining your deals. It is likely that many deals will disappear if you have to accumulate a $35 order to qualify for Free Super Saver Shipping.

Since Amazon Prime ships items out so quickly (usually within a few hours of ordering,) you can list your items immediately after you hit the "buy" button. If you want to be extra careful, you can wait until the item ships before listing it on eBay.

Purchases and sales move so quickly during the fourth quarter that I have often sold items on eBay minutes after pushing the "buy" button on Amazon. All I then had to do was wait for the package to arrive within the next 2 days, remove the packing slip and reship it out with a new label!

15 RETAIL VS ONLINE SOURCES

There are pros and cons to buying either from online or retail sources. While you may appear to be buying something from the same company, for example Staples' brick and mortar store and staples.com, the deals and processes of purchasing something online may be different from making that same purchase in store.

In the case of Staples, the advantages to purchasing at retail include being able to stack more coupons to get a better deal (success rate will depend on the store), and possibly being able to grab that last clearance item that nobody else noticed or wanted. Disadvantages include limited inventory and the time and effort needed to go to the store.

Advantages to purchasing online include higher inventory quantities in general, and having items packed and shipped directly to your door. Many online retailers offer free shipping on higher priced orders which saves you time and effort.

The downside in most cases is a longer shipping lead time. Sometimes, by the time your item arrives, the market for the item may have changed. Returns from online sources may also be harder, especially if you have to incur return shipping costs.

Be aware that many corporations run their online stores quite separately from their brick and mortar storefronts. In some cases, orders made online have to be returned by mail, that is, you cannot return the item to your local store. In other cases, even though the storefront may accept returns for items purchased online, the system is so separate that it makes the return process a big pain. Sam's Club is a good example of this problem.

16 REDUCING RISK

One distinct advantage of sourcing for items from retailers is that you can return items that do not sell. While I do not encourage the abuse of a store's return policy, it is certainly a factor in determining your risk level when you are making your purchases.

The retailers that I mentioned in this book have average to outstanding return policies. Some do not even have a time-limit on returns. However, to be fair, I suggest that you do not hold on to an item for more than a year. Always keep your receipts. You will need it both for tax purposes, and in the event that you need to make a return.

Every now and then, you may lose a receipt or you may have accidentally missed the return window. Stores like Costco can pull up your purchase from your membership number. Some stores will accept returns without receipt. Many stores also allow returns without receipt immediately after the Christmas season.

Please do not abuse any store's return policy. Think of it more as a life-line than as a matter of the course of your business. Companies like Amazon have a history of banning customers who have had too many returns.

Deciding Your Margins

At this point in the book, you should have an idea of what items you can look out for to resell on eBay. You have found the item, and you have decided that you will be able to ship this item without much problem. Now, you need to decide if it is *profitable* enough to resell on eBay. Remember that eBay and Paypal will take a total of ~15% in fees and commissions.

The following sections of this chapter are guidelines which have worked for *me*. These may or may not work for *you*. It is more important for you to learn and know the fee structures of eBay and Paypal and how it relates to your situation. You will need to decide for yourself what works for you depending on your situation and risk-tolerance.

Average Margins That I Expect

How I normally decide if something is worth reselling is if I can get a 100% return in the sale price. That is, if I bought something for $50, I need to fairly confidently be able to resell the item on eBay for $100.

This would give me a big enough of a margin to cover my costs, fees and commissions while still returning a decent profit margin. It also gives me enough of a margin cushion to lower my price a little if needed.

Lower Margins On Easy-Sale/Low Risk Items

If something is fairly cheap and has a high demand on eBay, I may decide to accept a lower profit margin to make a few quick bucks since the risk is lower. You will find that packing and shipping will take up a large portion of your eBay time.

Because I know this, I may also accept a lower profit margin to resell something from Amazon because I know I would not have to worry about repackaging the shipment.

Higher Margins On Heavy and/or Bulky Items

Conversely, if something like a generator or barbecue set has a good resale potential, I may not purchase it for resale unless I have an expected 200-300% return, simply because of the logistics associated with transporting, packing and shipping such heavy and/or bulky items.

Margins on High Fraud Items

High fraud items are usually high-priced items including more expensive electronics and expensive, fine jewelry or other precious items. An iPad, for example, will be a high fraud item. Deciding on your profit margin threshold will depend on you. High fraud items like expensive electronics normally also sell well and sell quickly. They are usually easy to pack and ship.

In light of these factors, I normally decide on accepting a *lower* margin because of the ease of sale. To protect myself, I will restrict sales to within the US, or within developed countries only. I will also invest in shipping insurance. It is cheaper to purchase insurance through U-PIC (http://u-pic.com) or ShipSaver (http://shipsaver.com) than through the USPS.

If you are using UPS or Fedex, just purchase any additional insurance you need to via either of those carriers. If the item is more than $250, you should also use a signature on delivery service. Paypal will not protect sellers for purchases above $250 (including shipping). If there is a dispute, Paypal will only offer you seller protection if you shipped the item using signature delivery service.

However, if I feel like I am not liquid enough at that time, I will decide that I need a higher margin on a high-fraud risk item.

If you are offering free shipping on the item, make sure you have that carefully figured out before you try to resell the item. Remember: miscalculating a free shipping offer can quickly turn your profitable sale into a loss-making venture.

My main take-home message in this chapter is simple - if you do not feel comfortable selling the item, be it for shipping or fraud or margin reasons - DON'T! There is no need to overthink a purchase. There will be plenty of other opportunities to resell something else.

17 LISTING DESCRIPTIONS

Item Condition

I cannot emphasize how important it is to have your items accurately and thoroughly described. It is especially important to describe your items properly if you are selling collectible items. Your item is "brand new" if it is sealed and never-been opened.

An item can be "brand new" but with "shelf-wear". Meaning that it is new and sealed but the box could be dinged or torn from wear while being on the store shelf. Shelf-worn brand new items would normally apply to items you may have purchased from thrift stores or places like TJ Maxx and Tuesday Morning. Clearance items can also be shelf-worn.

"Like-New" could be an item that has been opened but never used. For example, a video game set that I broke apart to sell the disc-only would be a "like-new" disc. You can also state that the disc has never been used but came from a collector set that you sold separately.

After bad experiences in my early years selling Anime trading cards, I never ever call any item I sell "mint". Mint really means "mint". Buyers who buy your "mint" item will expect it to be mint.

They will nit-pick any flaw that you did not notice. Be very careful about using this term unless you are an expert in grading. You will also need to describe any flaws or anything else that apply to your item. If in doubt, post pictures of any problems with the item.

Any refurbished, open-box or return items that you are selling should be stated as such. If you are selling refurbished or open-box items, I advise you to purchase the extended warranty from the retailer. Make sure that the warranty is easily transferrable and include it with the item.

You can factor the price of the warranty into the eBay price. If applicable, include in your description that the item includes a transferable extended warranty and that the buyer should refer to the warranty issuer if any problems with the item arises.

Pre-Sale Listings

If you want to list presale items, you must meet all of the following criteria:

- Guarantee that the item will be available for shipping within 30 days from the purchase date. Be sure to clearly state this information in your listing.
- Clearly indicate in the listing that the item is a presale item.
- The handling time specified in your listing should reflect the time from the end of the listing until the item is shipped to the buyer. Be sure to specify the correct handling time in your listing.

Make sure your listing follows these guidelines. If it doesn't, it may be removed, and you may be subject to a range of other actions, including limits of your buying and selling privileges and suspension of your account.

Shipping Policy

Include your shipping policy clearly. If you can only ship once a week, state this clearly. It would be even better if you told your customers that you can only ship items on, for example, Tuesday afternoons. If you can, include an explanation for this shipping policy, for example, if you are unable to drive and your neighbor kindly takes you into town every Tuesday.

If you ship everyday, say so, for example, orders that are received by 1pm MST will ship the same business day, if not, it will ship the next business day. Give yourself some breathing room by letting your customers know that you are just one person and from time to time, shipments may be delayed for unexpected reasons and thank them for their patience and understanding.

If you used my profit-maximizing tricks of using recycled packaging, you might also want to include that in this section. You can state something like: "In order to reduce waste and help keep prices as low as possible for my customers, I use only recycled packaging materials. Thank you for your understanding and for helping save the environment."

Having a clear shipping policy is extremely important, especially during the fourth quarter. As I mentioned in the earlier chapter, customers are extremely sensitive to shipping times during this period. You should strive to ship items within the next business day during the fourth quarter.

The closer you get to Christmas, the more quickly you will need to ship.

If you want to take advantage of the Christmas shopping rush, I suggest that you also offer priority mail and express mail shipping options. Many people are willing to pay more for these shipping upgrades during this time.

You should be prepared by stocking up on USPS Priority Mail and Express Mail supplies. The USPS will supply you with all kinds of boxes. They will even give you packing tape! Have all these in hand. You can always return your excess boxes to your local Post Office after the season ends.

Return Policy

Your return policy should be clearly stated in your item description. The next question you might be wondering is, should you accept returns? That it is up to you. Some sellers may claim that your sales would improve if you offer a return policy.

Honestly, I have not seen any difference in sales whether or not I accept returns. Simply put, no, I do not accept returns. I am not Walmart or some big corporation. Just as you do not expect a garage sale seller to accept returns, I do not feel that my buyers should expect me to accept returns.

Since almost all the items I sell are brand new and sealed, there should be no reason for a return unless there is a manufacturing defect in the item, at which time I will accept a return. However, these instances are rare. The only other reason I would accept a return is if I made a mistake in the description. For example, if I stated by accident that the item is brand new when it was actually a refurbished item.

Regardless of whether you decide to accept returns or not, always be extremely explicit in your terms. For example you can say, "All sales are final unless there is a manufacturing defect. The buyer is responsible for any return shipping costs."

18 COMETH THE TAX MAN

Disclaimer: This chapter is for general informational purposes only and should not be construed as professional advice. Please seek a local tax or legal professional for advice specific to your situation.

When you start selling on eBay as a business, you will need to run your business like a business. That also means that you can also receive the tax benefits of running a business. In order to maximize profits, you will also need to try to minimize your tax liabilities (legally).

Be sure to save all your receipts. Your main business costs will include eBay and paypal fees and commissions, inventory and supply costs, shipping and packing costs. Buying club or warehouse club memberships can be included if you are using the services for your business.

Other costs can include milage, gas, parking and vehicle wear expenses. Do not forget your overhead expenses! For most eBay sellers, this can include a home office, computers, internet and phone service etc.

The IRS will allow you to deduct the percentage of personal items that you use for your business. For example, I use about 25% of my home for my eBay business. That includes a dedicated home office and dedicated areas for eBay supply storage. I can deduct 25% of my utility and home mortgage expenses as a business expense.

Again, this is not tax or financial advice. please consult your tax professional for advice for your specific situation.

I use an accordion folder to keep all my receipts in order. To keep track of vehicle mileage, I also have a little notebook that I use to note the mileage of every eBay-buying trip I make. At the end of the year, I take the miles used for business and divide it by the total miles traveled to get the vehicle wear/expenses and gas cost for my eBay-ing.

You can also consider using apps like Outright (http://ebay.to/1rd7UQJ) which is a paid subscription service, or GoDaddy Bookkeeping (http://bit.ly/1np6wPw) which is free.

You might also find Quickbooks helpful. Quickbooks is not free but you can often get it free after rebate at Staples or Office Depot/OfficeMax. If you decide on using Quickbooks, keep an eye out for a free-after-rebate offer on Slickdeals.

19 CONCLUSION

I hope you found this book helpful. Whether you want to make selling on eBay a hobby, a side-income business or a full-time business, you can adopt some or all of my profit-maximizing ideas.

Again, this book is meant to be a tool - my way of teaching you how to fish, rather than giving you a fish. Be flexible. Deal-hunting and eBay selling is not for everyone. Fashion this tool to suit your needs and most importantly, HAVE FUN!

Like my books? Sign up at http://byjillbcom to receive three FREE e-books:
The Modern American Frugal Housewife
Can Dos and Don'ts
How to Keep Backyard Chickens

Disclaimer: This guide is for entertainment and informational purposes only. The author and anyone associated with this book shall not be held liable for damages incurred through the use of information provided herein. Content included on this book is not intended to be, nor does it constitute, the giving of financial, legal or professional advice.

The author and others associated with this book make no representation as to the accuracy, completeness or validity of any information in this book. While every caution has been taken to provide the most accurate information, please use your own discretion before making any decisions based solely on the content herein.

The author and others associated with this book are not liable for any errors or omissions nor will provide any form of compensation if you suffer an inconvenience, loss or damages of any kind because of, or by making use of, the information contained herein. Any opinion given is the author's own, based on her experience. If in doubt, always seek the advice of a professional who can advise you appropriately before acting on any part of this book.

This book contains references and links to other Third Party products and services. Some of these references have been included for the convenience of the readers and to make the book more complete. They should not be construed as endorsements from, or of any of these Third Parties or their products or services. These links and references may contain products and opinions expressed by their respective owners. The author does not assume liability or responsibility for any Third Party material or opinions.

Books By Jill b.

Please check out my other books at **http://byjillb.com**:

The Modern Frugal American Housewife Book #1
Home Economics

The Modern Frugal American Housewife Book #2
Organic Gardening

The Modern Frugal American Housewife Book #3
Moms Edition

The Modern Frugal American Housewife Book #4
Emergency Prepping

CAN Dos and Don'ts
Water Bath and Pressure Canning

How to Keep Backyard Chickens
A Straightforward Beginner's Guide

The Best Backyard Chicken Breeds
A List of Top Birds for Pets, Eggs and Meat

Foraging
A Beginner's Guide to Wild Edible and Medicinal Plants

Medicinal Herb Gardening
10 Plants for The Self-Reliant Homestead Prepper

How to Make Money on eBay: Beginner's Guide

From Setting Up Accounts to Selling Like a Pro

How to Make Money on eBay: Maximize Profits

Secrets, Stories, Tips and Hacks - Confessions of a 16-Year eBay Veteran

How to Make Money on eBay: International Sales

Taking the Fear and Guesswork Out of Doing Business Internationally on eBay

Self-Publish on a Budget with Amazon

A Guide for the Author Publishing eBooks on Kindle

ABOUT THE AUTHOR

HomeGrown • HomeMade • HomeBusiness • HOMESTEAD

Jill b. is an author, entrepreneur, homesteader and is the co-inventor and co-founder of Chicken Armor (http://chickenarmor.com), an affordable, low maintenance chicken saddle. She has also written over a dozen homesteading and home business books.

With a no-nonsense style, Jill draws from her own experiences and mistakes, and writes books focusing on maximizing output with minimal input to save you time and money.

Jill has been mentioned/quoted in various publications including The Associated Press, The New York Times, The Denver Post and ABC News. She has written for various magazines including Countryside and Small Stock Journal, Molly Green, Farm Show Magazine and Backyard Poultry Magazine. She holds an Engineering degree from an Ivy League from a previous life.

At its height, her homestead included over 100 chickens, geese and ducks, as well as cats, a dog, bees and a donkey named Elvis. She currently lives on her homestead in rural Oregon.

Learn more by visiting her site http://byjillb.com.